"Kristopher Norris has crafted a witty, exegetically astute, and even prophetic riff on the book of James. His hopeful and insatiable passion for the church is evident on every page. Norris's text captures the true soul of James' letter, an exercise in orthopraxy that is direct, challenging, pragmatic, and missionally 'spot on' for the church in its present cultural context."

—TIM CONDER
Founding Pastor of Emmaus Way in Durham, North Carolina,
and author of *Free for All: Rediscovering the Bible in Community*

"With the cultural disestablishment of Christianity in America in full swing, churches are being forced to come to terms with what it means to live in a world where they no longer enjoy privileged standing. As Christendom declines Christians have the opportunity to learn apostolic faith and practice anew by identifying with the image of the church as a pilgrim people in a strange land. Yet knowing this new reality and living into it are different matters. This book offers basic training for equipping churches to embrace their identity as a community of pilgrims and to embark on the missional journey."

—CURTIS W. FREEMAN
Research Professor of Theology and
Director of the Baptist House of Studies,
Duke University Divinity School

"With writing as vivid and engaging as his vision of the Church, Kris Norris opens up fresh sky over what it means to follow Jesus in the world. I already want to read it again."

—JULIE PENNINGTON-RUSSELL
Pastor, First Baptist Church, Decatur, GA

"*Pilgrim Practices: Discipleship for a Missional Church*, like the book of James on which it is based, is full of wisdom and passion. It is a poignant and powerful explanation of Christian discipleship, offering a compelling journey guide for individuals to follow Jesus in the context of missional communities. I especially appreciated the clear call to engage in 'practices' that form identity and define what it means to be fully human."

—DANIEL VESTAL
Executive Coordinator, Cooperative Baptist Fellowship

"A refreshing and honest look at two critical ingredients for a New Testament church in our twenty-first-century world . . . missional discipleship. What is it? How can it happen? Who are those to lead the way? The answers are discovered through the author's walk through the Letter of James. A worthy read that can empower missional leaders and churches."

—EDWARD HAMMETT
Author of *Reframing Spiritual Formation: Discipleship in an Unchurched Culture*

Pilgrim Practices

DISCIPLESHIP FOR A MISSIONAL CHURCH

Kristopher Norris

CASCADE *Books* · Eugene, Oregon

PILGRIM PRACTICES
Discipleship for a Missional Church

Copyright © 2012 Kristopher Norris. All rights reserved. Except for brief quotations in critical publications or reviews, no part of this book may be reproduced in any manner without prior written permission from the publisher. Write: Permissions, Wipf and Stock Publishers, 199 W. 8th Ave., Suite 3, Eugene, OR 97401.

Cascade Books
An Imprint of Wipf and Stock Publishers
199 W. 8th Ave., Suite 3
Eugene, OR 97401

www.wipfandstock.com

ISBN 13: 978-1- 61097-865-1

New Revised Standard Version Bible, copyright 1989, Division of Christian Education of the National Council of the Churches of Christ in the United States of America. Used by permission. All rights reserved.

Cataloging-in-Publication data:

Norris, Kristopher.

   Pilgrim practices : discipleship for a missional church / by Kristopher Norris.

   xviii + 142 p. ; 23 cm. — Includes bibliographical references and indexes.

   ISBN 13: 978-1-61097-865-1

   1. Christian Life. 2. Spiritual life—Christianity. I. Title.

BV4501.3 N664 2012

Manufactured in the U.S.A.

To my grandmothers,
who showed me what disciples look like

Contents

Acknowledgments

I CAN ONLY BEGIN these acknowledgements by acknowledging that I am in a position to be able to write a book—even a book attempting to show that the Bible enjoins us to give up possessions, live peaceably, and offer risky hospitality, among other radical endeavors. While I do believe Scripture commands these practices of everyone, I recognize that my position of relative social and economic privilege allows me the resources and opportunity to research and write about them and perhaps enables me to more easily advocate them. I try to be aware of this in all that I write. There are many folks who have more profundity and insight than I do but who are not in a situation allowing them to write a book. I hope this work shares their concerns and thoughts.

Secondly, I must acknowledge that this book is not a "solo project." Rather, in keeping with its primary theme, this is a collaborative work of Christian community. These thoughts about theology and scripture were generated from innumerable conversations with many insightful friends who deserve much gratitude. This book has been on a long and arduous journey of several years. I am grateful to Charlie Collier and the folks at Wipf and Stock for rescuing it from the depths of the abyss just when all hope seemed lost and to Rodney Clapp for taking on this editing responsibility at the last minute. I especially want to thank Jonathan Wilson Hartgrove and Steve Harmon for their generosity and hospitality in helping to make this connection. In addition to these formal collaborators, I owe a great deal to other friends. John Veazey and Amy Canosa are the two best amateur (and *pro bono*) editors one could ask for. Curtis Freeman was instrumental in reviewing several instantiations of this manuscript, offering insights, and redirecting me when needed—right up

Acknowledgments

until the end—and deserves many thanks. Tim Conder, Daniel Vestal, and AJ Walton also read and commented on significant portions of this manuscript. I'm grateful to you all!

While I am a product of all the churches I have attended and ministered with, I would like to thank two explicitly: Fairview Baptist for raising me to understand that church is important and for forming me in a way that values community, Scripture, and a commitment to the life of discipleship; and Hope Fellowship, where this book began. Finally, I thank my family and especially my parents, Keith and Elizabeth, for their continual love and encouragement of my calling as a minister. From the time I was young they have tolerated and supported my writing: Daddy encouraged and believed in me and Mama began writing down my "stories" before I was even old enough to do so myself. I love you.

Foreword

I WRITE THIS WHILE sitting in a near-empty airport lobby, pondering another in a long line of too many geographical transitions in too few years. I've found there is hardly a more lonesome occasion than flying alone and waiting in a vacant, modest-sized airport as the day drifts into night. The milky grey sky outside the window casts a gloomy hue across the terminal. A few passersby walk silently past one another with scarcely a glance, much less a smile or word of greeting. The temperature and atmosphere are chilly. Interrupted only by the occasional crackling announcement from the intercom, I sketch these words on a notepad. A place I've often thought of as one of joyous reunions, exhilarating expeditions, and refreshing escapes—a place where people embark on great journeys together—on this night the airport is one of preoccupied encounters, solitary shadows, and unsettling quiet.

I also write this several weeks into the season of Easter, a few days from Pentecost—the day Christians celebrate the birth of the church. Pentecost commemorates the day God's Spirit came down among the gathered disciples as tongues of fire, not resting on one single person but on "all together in one place." The Spirit filled the crowded room of the house, and the disciples began speaking ecstatically in the languages of every nation, so that all could hear and understand the good news. This unsettling raucousness and joyous union across ethnic, national, and social lines marked the beginning of the church, the rebirth of the Body of Christ in the world. This was a Body undistinguished by language, color, gender, economic status, or national citizenship, but a Body of people now on a mission together, constituted by a Way of life together.

This is a book about that Way of life, lived together in the church community, a movement set in motion by God for God's people. *Pilgrim*

Practices explores a certain understanding of what it means to be disciples of Jesus Christ—to find one's identity in him and with each other, and to constitute a mission through particular and peculiar practices derived from the story and message of Scripture. This is a book about discipleship for a church that is missional, a church that seeks to remain faithful to God's mission and calling in a swiftly changing time and landscape that make it difficult to do so. In the pages that follow I hope many of you will discover, rediscover, or simply appreciate a love for the church, for Scripture, for Christian practices of faith, and for the tremendous adventure God calls us to share together as a witness and blessing for the world.

This is a book both *from* and *for* the church. In fact, it was during my first months as a fledgling pastor that I saw the need for more intensive discipleship formation, and it was during this time that the impetus for this project developed. The concept of the project and a few of the chapters evolved from a sermon series I preached when I first began pastoral ministry with a new congregation. I titled the series, "What does it mean to be the church?" These sermons gave our fellowship a common language from which to begin as we examined what it meant to be God's church and how God was calling us to participate in God's mission in the world. After a couple years of extensive work, thematic reframing, and incessant tweaking, my hope is that this book might do the same for you and your congregation.

Throughout this book I will share more of myself—formative stories, struggles, and insights. I firmly believe you cannot separate content from context, so I cannot help placing some of myself within these pages. I also hope to introduce you to some of the Christian thinkers and writers who have been important and influential for me. The endnote citations will provide a rich bibliography of theologians and ministers and their writings that articulate these important points far better than I can do here. Some of the endnotes offer more depth into particular points, issues, or quotations for the more theologically curious reader. I have also placed a Discussion Guide at the end for readers who want to use this book as a resource for small groups, retreats, congregational leadership, or other groups.

Kristopher Norris
Pentecost, 2010

Introduction

Community in a *Survivor* Culture

THE BLUE AND RED neon light of the "Open" sign was strangely warm and welcoming. As we opened the glass doors to step inside the Waffle House, we were greeted by the muddled scents of fried bacon, burnt coffee, and maple syrup. I was tired, hungry, and cranky. My three friends and I were beginning our road trip back to North Carolina from a brief vacation in Florida, and we had decided to start our overnight drive with a late visit to one of my favorite restaurants. We would soon be cramped in my compact car, taking turns driving along fourteen hours of stiff, dull interstate through the middle of the night—but for now, just waffles, thick syrup, greasy bacon, and cheesy, tossed, sliced, diced, any-way-you-like-them hash browns. A temporary taste of heaven!

The four of us crowded into one of the small window booths, and as we sat in silence, eyes dazed and stomachs growling, I did what I always do when I go to a diner late at night. I people-watched. I like to think of the Waffle House as the great social equalizer. It doesn't matter if you are rich, poor, white, black, brown, gay, straight, hippie, yuppie, geeky, happy, or melancholy—everyone enjoys a visit to the Waffle House. I saw a few young people sitting at the counter, one wearing flowery board shorts and a sleeveless shirt, probably college students coming back from spring break at the beach. Two men pulled up on bikes, one with an eyebrow piercing and a green mohawk, the other with a shaved head and stylish black-rimmed eyeglasses. They sat down, pulled out worn notebooks, and began journaling as they ordered coffee. At the far end, a young lady in a sundress sitting at a booth alone stood up and announced cheerfully to the entire restaurant that her boyfriend had just proposed. With a contagious grin she suggested we play a song for her on the jukebox to celebrate. As she stood dancing by herself to a golden oldie love song, our waitress revealed that the young lady's husband had recently died. She often came into this restaurant—a place she and her husband frequented—with illusions that he was still there with her. As our steamy food arrived, I saw more travelers enter the restaurant, weary from a long and late day of travel to some far-off destination and desperate for a respite from the monotonous journey.

Besides polite obligatory greetings, no one spoke to each other. Most people generally ignored the odd girl at the jukebox or looked cautiously at the mohawked fellow at the bar. People came in to take a rest from their belabored lives or activities, to have their stomachs filled, to listen to a few good tunes, and to be shortly back on their respective ways.

As I sat in the booth talking with my friends, I was distracted by thoughts of the church—one of the pitfalls of being a minister, I guess. In many ways, I thought, Christians in North America view church as we do a Waffle House. Churches are a place of rest and rehab, a break from the difficulties of life. We come, tired and disillusioned from life's journey, seeking nourishment—often spiritual and sometimes physical (especially if your church is like mine and loves the post-worship potluck!). We come into the place as individuals, from our own private lives and disparate locations, and then leave to continue on our individual journeys, feeling rested, full, and rejuvenated for the next week's tasks. There is no common goal, no common community, no common journey among the weary travelers at a Waffle House, and unfortunately, the same thing is often true of our churches.

Changes in Longitude, Changes in Attitude

For years pastors, pollsters, and academics have been signaling the death of the church, or at least the death of the church as we know it.[1] Church attendance in most North American denominations is plummeting. The percentage of people attending church has dropped dramatically in the past sixty years while more and more young people are growing up outside of church.[2] In fact, the number of those who identify themselves as

Christian has dropped nearly 15 percent over that same period. One-half of American adults do not attend church, and every day we encounter people of other faiths at the grocery store, at work, or right next door. In the United States, we can hardly say that we live in a "Christian society."

All this is at a time when other reports say the United States is one of the most religious nations on earth and becoming even more religious.[3] Americans are becoming more religious, but at the same time church attendance (as well as attendance at houses of worship for other faiths) is swiftly falling. Why the paradox?

Modern western culture is changing at a rapid pace. Technology and information are growing exponentially. People today have the capabilities to travel to countries across the world in a day, and also to destroy countries across the world in a day. As society becomes more globalized, allowing instant connections with businesses or people all over the world, people at the same time become more isolated. Communications scholar Quentin Schultz noted, "Oddly enough, in our world of abundant messaging, we are losing both our memories and communities. As information technology mediates the world for us, we have less direct association with others, and we consequently lose our own sense of interdependence."[4] Studies show that more people are choosing to live alone while greater emphasis is placed on individual achievement. For example, think about popular TV shows—*Survivor, The Bachelor, The Apprentice,* or my personal favorite *I'm a Celebrity, Get Me Out of Here.* In each of these shows, people are placed into a community where they work together, but only so that in the end each individual can defeat all the others. These "reality" shows represent the reality of our culture.

The allure of success and the glorification of freedom have dominated modern American culture, and while most Americans long for community, we feel the pressure to succeed on our own at any cost. We have countless options for anything in life—different options for lattes at Starbucks, endless shopping options one click away on the Internet, burgers "my way" at Burger King. And we would be blind if we thought these changes in society didn't affect religion as well. Drive down the street in a reasonably sized town and you will encounter endless religious options. Different faith traditions, different denominations, different worship styles, different mission emphases, and different ways of attracting people to come into the doors. Churches accommodate the needs and desires of the individual because that is the only way to survive. America can be more religious at the same time that church attendance is dropping not because people have lost their faith but because their faith has become more privatized. I can practice faith on my own. Rather than a devaluing of faith, this is a devaluing of community and commitment to a common journey. Under the weighty influence of modernism, combined with American sentiments of free enterprise and autonomy, we live in a time of extreme individualism ubiquitous in all areas of life, especially religion.[5]

So What's the Point?

In many ways, churches in North America have lost the original, radical sense of community; the original, radical sense of common mission; the original, radical sense of discipleship. This book is a meager effort at the retrieval of these things, which in a sense are one thing altogether. This book examines discipleship for a missional church through the framework of two fundamental Christian concepts—pilgrimage and practice. (I purposefully avoided the language of "reexamining" or "reframing" discipleship because this is not a new understanding but an ancient and simple one.) The purpose of this book is to introduce certain practices to help Christians and churches in their mutual life of discipleship. My aim is to frame discipleship in a way that has been largely abandoned in modern congregational literature; that is, I advocate for an understanding of discipleship as fundamentally an issue of identity that is necessarily formed and lived in community with others. Simplified, discipleship is primarily an identity and is formed and practiced in and through the church community.

Discipleship is a lifestyle that cannot be lived on one's own, and being a disciple ultimately means engaging with others on a journey of faith sustained and cultivated through pilgrim practices. The practices examined in this book, what I call pilgrim practices, develop and direct the pilgrimage of Christians, transforming them into disciples—as the Body of Christ—who participate with God in God's mission in the world. To be clear, this is not two distinct pilgrimages—one of developing disciples and the other of participating in God's global mission. Rather, it is one continuous pilgrim journey. In other words, identity formation and missional engagement are simultaneous events on the Christian pilgrimage.

There is not some magical point of transition where a person becomes a full-fledged disciple or a community becomes the Body of Christ (although I do believe it is important that somewhere in the journey each disciple makes an intentional commitment to Jesus Christ through the Body of Christ). The same pilgrim practices that form and develop disciples also witness to the world of God's mission. They are both formative and missional.

This book, however, will focus primarily on the formation of disciples through these pilgrim practices. While the eight practices of this book certainly offer a witness to the world, I will highlight the ways they can form the church into a community of disciples on a common pilgrimage. Discipleship formation seems to be an area of struggle for many churches in the United States, often due to the restricting of discipleship to the confines of Christian education. I hope this book offers specific practices to help Christians form their identity as disciples and to help Christian communities live their calling as the Body of Christ in the world.[6]

Travel Log

This book is structured according to two parts. Part I, "Pilgrims on the Way," introduces the primary themes in laying the groundwork for a proper discussion of pilgrim practices. Chapter 1 explores why pilgrimage is an important theme for imagining the church, and why practices are essential for supporting the church on its pilgrimage. It explains the way James will be used as a guide for this journey into pilgrim practices. Chapters 2 and 3 place the themes of pilgrimage and practice directly within the life of the Christian community. In chapter 2, I focus on the church by examining biblical images for church and positioning the congregation as the essential context for discipleship. Chapter 3 explores the idea of "missional church" through the lens of Luke's description of the early church in Acts 2, situating pilgrim practices within the church's participation in God's mission.

After introducing these themes, Part II examines eight specific pilgrim practices. With James as the guidebook, eight practices emerge that shape and form discipleship in a missional community. Each chapter focuses on one of the eight pilgrim practices emerging from one of the eight key sections in James's letter.

Introduction

There are many books available on doctrine, on missions, or on congregational programs, and these are both important and necessary. But in this strange time of transient identities and fleeting commitments, contemporary Christians do not need more books telling us what to do as much as prophets to tell us who we are! James is such a prophet, offering images that cast a new vision, instill a new reality, and reveal to us our true identity. Discipleship is more than an educational program or a list of obligations; it is primarily an identity requiring a pilgrimage of transformation that cannot be developed apart from the church community (Rom 12:2).

PART I

Pilgrims on the Way

1

The Pilgrim Road, or
Why Practices Matter

ONE OF MY FAVORITE scenes in the Lord of the Rings movie trilogy comes near the beginning of the first film, *The Fellowship of the Ring*.[1] Frodo and Sam are embarking on their journey to return the dangerous ring to the volcanic region of Mordor in order to destroy it. As they are leaving the Shire and walking through a cornfield, suddenly Sam stops. Frodo asks him if there is a problem, and Sam replies that if he takes one more step it will be the farthest from the Shire he has ever ventured. As Frodo recalls Bilbo's words to him as a youngster, "It is a dangerous business, Frodo, going out of your door," Sam and Frodo pause in a moment of reflection, fear, and anticipation, knowing that they are on a journey after which they will never be the same again.

As Christians, we also think of life as a journey. This idea has become popularized in recent books, articles, sermons, and curriculum. The popularity of "missional" language, emphasizing the "sent-ness" of God's people out into the world, heightens this metaphor of journey. It is not a new concept, however. Christian heroes from Teresa of Avila to John Bunyan spoke of the Christian life as a journey toward God. Whether understood as a voyage out into the world or inward toward the center of God (or both simultaneously), this metaphor has helped Christians understand what it means to be a follower of Christ for centuries. Stopping with the concept of a mystical or missional journey, however, fails to describe all that it means to be a disciple. Disciples are not on individualized excursions with occasional refresher stops at the local waffle joint or sanctuary of their choice. They are not on impulsive road trips or aimless wanderings to try to find themselves. Instead, they are on a journey of anticipation with an established destination. As Sam and Frodo understand at the beginning of their journey, standing at the edge of all they have known, it is both a choice they make and a journey to which they are called, a formative and transformative adventure that binds people to one another in unique and imaginative ways. In this way, disciples are better understood as traveling on a pilgrimage.

Pilgrim Progress

Most religions historically required some form of transition from one stage of development to another, and in this vein, they developed certain rites of passage. While some of us may feel the urge to seclude some of the teenagers in our churches indefinitely, ancient tribal religions often secluded young initiates or removed them from the village for a time in order to aid in their religious transition. Christianity and Judaism developed rituals such as catechisms or bar/bat mitzvahs. For most religions, these transitions incorporate some form of marginalization from dominant society, a detachment or separation from a social structure or cultural conditions.[2] Anthropologists Victor and Edith Turner note that Christianity also generated its ritual transition, especially during the Middle Ages, in the practice of pilgrimage to a sacred site or shrine.

On vacation in Rome a few years ago, I remember walking miles through the historic districts from my hotel to visit two churches, one that claimed to hold St. Paul's head (evidently sealed in gold after being beheaded in what is now St. Peter's Square) and the other a piece of Jesus' cross. (In full disclosure, I also visited a church that claimed to hold the finger of St. Thomas that touched the scars on Jesus' hands and side!) While these artifacts may seem odd or even grotesque to those of us with modern religious sensibilities, hundreds of years ago Christian pilgrims made long and dangerous journeys to worship at such sacred sites. These pilgrim journeys "cut across boundaries of provinces, realms, and even empires," note the Turners, involving much danger and sacrifice.[3] Hunger, disease, thieves, and fatigue all complicated the pilgrim journey. The pilgrim had to be ready to sacrifice health, money, safety, and even life for the sake of the goal. For this reason, pilgrims found it imperative to travel together—not only because companionship made the journey more enjoyable but also because the danger of the course required solidarity, and the worship at the destination was best shared with others. Pilgrims traveled to the margins, physically and spiritually, in a journey of transition. They knew they would be constantly changing, never again the same, on this journey across territories; they also saw endless potential for redemption and renewal in this journey through time.

In this way, the concept of pilgrimage is essential for rightly understanding discipleship. While many of us may not journey to the ancient shrines of Rome or Jerusalem, the Christian life is a pilgrimage nonetheless. It is a journey not primarily through space but through time, with an end in sight. While some Christians identify this journey with the popular automaker slogan, "Enjoy the ride," the reason *pilgrimage* is a more beneficial and accurate portrayal of the Christian life and mission is that the Christian pilgrimage has an end. It is eschatological.[4] It is a journey *to* God and *of* God's mission that ultimately ends with the reign of God, with all things made new. Like medieval pilgrims, Christians must travel humbly and vulnerably in their difficult journey, relying on each other—and God's grace—for strength and sustenance, as well as the hospitality of other people of good will. Like medieval pilgrimages, discipleship is a journey of transformation, a sacred journey with others toward God's ultimate redemption of all humanity. In John Bunyan's classic, *The Pilgrim's Progress*, his protagonist, named Christian, journeys from the City of Destruction to the Celestial City with his companions Faithful and Hopeful. These travelers meet various temptations in the form of pernicious characters and perilous territories, from Talkative who hears and says but fails to "do" the word of God, to Mr. Worldy-Wiseman who seeks the short and easy way, to Apollyon the ruler of the earthly city who demands allegiance, to Mr. By-ends's gang who seeks after God only for their own blessing and gain. Despite the misdirection and distractions of these characters, the faithful pilgrims work out their faith together and encourage one another, even after Faithful's martyrdom. As he crosses the final barrier to the City, a deep and swift river, Christian realizes that he could not make the journey on his own, but only through the help of his companions.[5]

It is important to understand that this pilgrimage is not an individual undertaking but a communal endeavor; it is the church that is on pilgrimage, formed and sustained through practices, and the individual Christian is part of this communal journey. It is also important to understand that imagining the church as a community on pilgrimage is not a new conceptual framework. Its roots lie in God's description of the Israelites as strangers and aliens on their journey to the Promised Land (see Lev 19:34 among other references throughout the Torah). The Christian tradition has a rich heritage of pilgrim language, popularized by the ecclesial reflections of Augustine in the fourth century and his writings on the *civitate peregrinae*, the pilgrim city, in *The City of God*. In his ecclesiological study *Another City*, Barry Harvey noted of Augustine's work, "The members of this alternative ecclesia were always to remember that they were foreign visitors in the imperial city, and thus were to regard their dwellings as though they were tents, for ultimately they were pilgrims in this world, bearing witness in their bodies to another faith, another hope, another love."[6] The language of pilgrimage has become an important image for denoting the church's relationship with the world, ultimate eschatological orientation, and inclusion in God's mission of redeeming the world.

Like the ancient rites of passage, Christians participate in God's mission of redemption through practices involved in the pilgrimage. Diana Butler Bass describes a pilgrim as someone who "adopts a new place and new identity by learning a new language, rhythms, and practices." A person embarks on a pilgrimage "not to escape life, rather to embrace it more deeply, to be transformed wholly as a person with new ways of being in community and new hopes for the world."[7] The eschatological dimension of this journey means that we are not only experiencing something new but also becoming something new and making the world new in the process. As the Apostle Paul writes, "there is a new creation" (2 Cor 5:17).

Practice Makes Perfect?

In order to sustain the journey, any traveler must maintain certain practices. The Christian life necessitates specific practices to keep pilgrims on the path, moving toward the goal. The concept of Christian practices has gained much attention recently, in academic circles as the field of practical theology and in congregations as spiritual disciplines or practices of faith. From disciplines like *lectio divina* and labyrinth walking to ministry practices like evangelism or tithing, the idea of practices can denote many different things. In the context of discipleship and pilgrimage, I understand pilgrim practices to be activities in which the whole congregation engages. They are intentional patterns of life that direct the pilgrims as they participate in God, with each other, and for the world. Pilgrim practices are a way of life for a people who commit themselves to Jesus Christ as Lord.

Dorothy Bass and Miroslav Volf offered another helpful definition: "Christian practices are patterns of cooperative human activity in and through which life together takes shape over time in response to and in God as known in Jesus Christ."[8] This definition articulates several key components of practices as I understand them: they involve communal action and participation in God's mission, form a way of life for a people, and deal with social rather than individual activities.[9] They produce a place, such as church.[10] While Bass and Volf correctly noted that practices are certainly human activities, it is important to remember that these practices do not originate with humanity. Instead, practices like the ones examined in this book are activities God is already doing in the world. Pilgrim practices, therefore, are ways we imitate God's character in the world and thus participate in God's mission. In this way, they are missional, communal, distinctive, and formative actions. They constitute the way of life that shapes, crafts, and sustains Christian disciples because they define and transform identity.[11]

Developing this identity follows the same process as learning to play an instrument or a sport. It takes practice. Theologian Sam Wells, alluding to the philosopher Aristotle, compared discipleship to the development of virtue. "Virtues are derived from repeated practices that a community continually performs because it regards them as central to its identity," he noted.[12] For example, think about college basketball, where players are still learning and developing. I'm a Tar Heel basketball fan, so we could say it is similar to watching the development of a great point guard on the basketball court like Phil Ford, Kenny Smith, or Ty Lawson. As the one who initiates the plays, the point guard is an essential component to a team. Through constant practices, the point guard cultivates certain skills to help him on the court—skills to know which play to call and when, to see the floor on the fast break, and to know where and when to pass the ball to a teammate. These skills eventually become instinct. Basketball announcers sometimes say, "He is thinking too much on the court," implying that thinking is dangerous in the midst of a game. This is not an indictment on playing the game intelligently; rather, it indicates that good players no longer have to think about what they are doing—it is instinct. Once instinct takes over, the point guard is no longer a person who plays basketball. His identity is instead formed around being a leader of that team.

That is similar to the way practices form individuals and congregations along the pilgrim journey of discipleship. Being a disciple is not about thinking, "What would Jesus do in this situation?" Rather, practices of discipleship, in imitation of God's character, are developed through the corporate worship and life of the church until they become "second nature," so to speak.[13]

One's identity becomes wrapped up and wrapped in the story of Scripture and the life of the church through these practices. Wells used the helpful metaphor of Scripture as a "training manual," wherein disciples are shaped by the practices and instinctive habits of the community.[14] By reading Scripture, the church learns the story and then continues that story as if it is second nature because its identity is so wrapped up in that strange story of God's people. Christian identity is not located primarily in church statements, worship attendance, or where one falls on the liberal/conservative spectrum. It is located in particular and peculiar practices and commitments. In other words, Christianity is not something people only think, feel, or say. It is something people *do*.[15]

Before moving from this introductory discussion of pilgrim practices, I should explain one more important dimension. The work of philosopher Michel de Certeau adds a subversive dimension to this concept of practice. I have noted that practices are communal, missional, distinctive, and formative, but what makes them distinguished as pilgrim practices is their subversive nature. In his discussion of the ways people outside mainstream society use and reappropriate cultural items from dominant society, de Certeau offered the example of Native Americans' response to Spanish colonizers. While submitting to their conquerors, he noted, "the Indians nevertheless often made of the rituals, representations, and laws imposed on them something quite different from what their conquerors had in mind."[16] The "others" in a society—those not considered to be part of the dominant culture—reuse cultural products imposed on them by the power structure but do so in their own ways. In this way, de Certeau added, they "deflect its power." While perhaps not realizing it, he identified a significant feature of Christian practices, that of subversive identity and witness. One example of this from Scripture could be Jesus' taking a Roman coin with an image of Caesar and using it as a means to reaffirm to his followers that they belong to God, that they were created in and witnesses to God's image. Jesus took an everyday emblem of the dominant pagan empire oriented toward worshiping that image and reappropriated it to shape the identity of his community (Mark 12:13–17).

Similarly, pilgrim practices form the community of disciples into the Body of Christ, meaning into a society that is subversive or counter-cultural—distinct from the ways of the dominant consumerist, individualistic, tribal, and violent society of modern North America. These practices form a way of life that is different from the everyday practices of the rest of the world; or, in John Howard Yoder's words, they form "believers who for Jesus' sake do ordinary social things differently."[17] For example, Christians take the elements of a simple meal, bread and wine, and see new and subversive possibilities in them. For Christians, these ordinary elements are infused with the meaning and memory of Christ's life and death. The meal attests to the unity of the congregational Body as it eats the Body of Christ and witnesses to the alternative economic ethics of the church, where all are welcome to feast regardless of social or economic status (1 Cor 11:17–33). Through this meal, Christians affirm their commitment to Christ above all, reach out evangelically to those who are hungry, thirsty, or marginalized, and anticipate a future meal where everyone is welcome and everyone will have their fill. Therefore, the church may be *in* the world in these ordinary ways and submit to the powers of this world, but that does not mean the church's practices must conform to those of the world. It is through these pilgrim practices that the church embodies its discipleship, its calling to be the Body of Christ. The practices highlighted in this book all represent ways Christian pilgrims witness to their distinctive identity in Christ and in this way subvert the powers and principalities of the world.

I hope it is clear from the above descriptions that practices are not individual undertakings. Practices are communal habits, engaged intentionally both to form the community in ways appropriate to that community's mission and to witness to that mission. The pilgrim practices in this book are for a church that lives "'between the times' so the church can be the church, distinguished from the ways of the world."[18] James McClendon notes the "provisional nature" of the church as it peers toward an eschatological fulfillment that has not come to fruition. It is important to understand that the church is on pilgrimage not through space but through time, not from the secular "world" to some sacred space but through the secular to the *eschaton*—that is, the time of God's ultimate redemption. In this way, the church sees itself, as McClendon explained, in the framework of the biblical narrative and with a biblical expectation, knowing what God has done and looking forward to what God will do. The end is not here, and the church has not yet arrived in the fullness of the kingdom of God.

While we may not be perfect, it is important to remember that we do not travel blindly. We have a guidebook to send us forward and practices to mold us on the Way. Ours is a pilgrimage of anticipation, and while the travels may be difficult and we are surely prone to wander, it is important to remember that we are not alone. As Diana Butler Bass so pithily put it, "Practice may not make perfect, but it does appear to make pilgrims."[19]

A Guide for the Journey

These pilgrim practices are drawn from a long line of Christian traditions and, most important, Christian Scripture.[20] Scripture shapes the lives of Christians by guiding our pilgrimage. Jim Fodor uses the evocative metaphor of God working Scripture into the lives of faithful listeners in worship like yeast kneaded into dough, creating a brand-new substance.[21] In this notion of pilgrim practices, it is the Bible that connects our pilgrimage with the past while also directing its future in transformative ways. Contrary to many contemporary evangelical perspectives, Tim Conder and Dan Rhodes noted that the Bible is "not so much a step-by-step process on how to get saved but a thick, layered narrative that describes a new way of life."[22] The Bible does not posit a set of rigid rules but describes God's character and offers practices to guide our pilgrimage with God.

While Christians seem to love arguing about how to interpret the Bible rightly, when understood as the story of God and God's people, the Bible becomes more than a book to be debated by historical critics and inerrantists or used to condemn others. Instead, God's story becomes our story; it becomes kneaded into us, a part of who we are as pilgrims and who we are to become.

Acknowledging the eschatological character of the narrative of Scripture and the journey of the church—that is, looking to the future and the culmination of the church's journey in God's promise of a "new heaven and new earth" (Rev 21:4)—we would do a disservice to the Bible to view it merely as a map, charting the exact rules to live by or an exact path to follow. Instead, by reading the Bible narratively, as the story of God's people in Israel and the church through which we are a continuation of that story, we would more accurately understand the Bible, according to Barry Harvey, as the "travel itinerary" of God's people. The story of the Bible is "the story of their pilgrimage as strangers and foreigners through this world toward the kingdom of God."[23] Harvey defined itinerary as a distinct type of narrative offering symbolic representations of actions, for example by telling the stories of former travelers. In this way, the Bible is not like a GPS system, as I have sometimes heard it described ("go 1.2 miles and turn right on Main St.," in the automated voice of your choosing). It does not direct us exactly where to go nor does it offer step-by-step instructions for the journey. Instead, the Scriptures tell a story in a narrative, poetic, parabolic, or epistolary genre, and this story serves as a guide for pilgrimage—detailing the actions, the practices, that make for a faithful journey to a sacred destination.[24] This itinerary, the account of "the cloud of witnesses" of previous pilgrims like Abraham, Ruth, Mary, and Paul, serves as our guide for our travel, a guidebook for the pilgrimage. "They traveled way before us," Harvey noted, and "these stories, when taken together, provide us with a living and generative memory that guides us on our pilgrimage through this present age toward the eternal commonwealth whose founder and sovereign is the Triune God."[25] This living memory in Scripture forms Christian practice, and these practices constitute the performance of this itinerary.

Building on Harvey's helpful analogy, this book will explore the issue of discipleship in today's church by using the New Testament book of James as a "guidebook." When I would go on family vacations to a national park or historical site, we would secure a guidebook from the park rangers before setting out on our exploration of Yellowstone or Gettysburg. A guidebook identifies points of interest or important notices to help people maneuver through what could be confusing or dangerous territory. It contains symbols, stories of previous travelers, and images to help the traveler on his or her journey. Here, the book of James as our guidebook points out images and concepts that direct us on the common journey of discipleship—through quite possibly dangerous territory.

James offers many vivid and intriguing images to provide us with a path of identity formation that can only be followed in community. These images offer a vision and inspire imagination. In using such graphic and captivating images, James evokes specific pilgrim practices for the congregations reading his letter. For example, by detailing a story of political and social favoritism in worship, James urges his readers to engage in the practice of hospitality, or welcoming (see chapter 6, "Welcoming"). Through his illustrations and exhortations, James gives his readers—from the first congregations in the first-century Near East to today's congregations in the individualized, consumer culture of the United States—practices that shape and form communities into the church. They transform identity and shape a way of life for the Christian pilgrimage. The distinctive nature of James presents a unique framework in which to examine practices of discipleship. In short, James offers a great place to start, or perhaps expand, understandings of Christian practice.

Scripture serves as the guide-book, illuminating the practices necessary to sustain pilgrims on their faithful journey. As we turn to the book of James as a guide, we will uncover eight essential practices for the Christian pilgrimage, practices for both cultivating and sustaining a community on its pilgrimage to God. These practices are essential because the journey is not easy—it is a dangerous business, going out of your door! Just as Bunyan's characters Christian, Faithful, and Hopeful discovered the many dangers and temptations in the characters they met along the way, they endured the journey because of the important practices they developed—practices like faith, prayer, loyalty, hospitality, and heeding wise counsel—all practices outlined in the guide-book of James (and in the upcoming chapters) and constitutive of the difficult life of discipleship. As Mr. Worldly-Wiseman warns the pilgrim Christian as he begins his journey, "there is not a more dangerous and troublesome way in the world.[26]

2

"iChurch," or Why Church Matters

I CONFESS THAT I have a proclivity toward skepticism when it comes to the latest trendy gadget or clothing item. It is not that I'm a Luddite, sitting in a rocking chair, sipping sweet tea, reminiscing about the good ol' days, and judging every person I see walking the sidewalk speaking into a Bluetooth earpiece (although I am fond of both rocking chairs and sweet tea). I refused to purchase an iPod for the longest time. It ran counter to all my "anti-trendy" sentiments. With most new fads, be they "boat shoes," iPods, HDTVs, or any clothing that does not come from the local thrift store, I systematically tell my friends that these are products of our consumerist culture, that advertisers are duping them into unnecessary purchases, that they are being materialistic and over-consumptive, that it is silly and overpriced, and that I will *never, ever* buy one. However, usually a few months or years after the trendy item's breakthrough, I one day realize that it, in fact, is quite useful and not so overpriced and I just might need one. This is the way it was with the iPod. I finally gave in to the sweet temptation of music-on-demand, despite all my finest convictions.

While this may seem like a silly personal struggle, I believe iPods have become the essence of trends. iTunes, iTouches, iHomes, iGoogle, iPhones, and iPads—the "i" sensation seems ubiquitous. An iPod is enticing because it puts the individual in complete control; it is the epitome of individual autonomy. It accommodates my tastes, my likes, my dislikes. I can sit with four other people in a car or a room together, and we each can listen with our earphones on our iPods to our own music. Catch a theme here? It is whatever I want at my fingertips. I have complete control.

It seems we have become an "iSociety." As we become more isolated from each other through the busyness of our lives, through desires to succeed, through technology that promises community but delivers only imitations of community, faith suffers as Christian lives become isolated as well. In a culture of pluralism, free choice, escapism, and consumerism, this social isolation leads to a fragmentary faith identity and impotent churches full of religious consumers.

Christians in this sense are simply a collection of individuals all seeking to make a local church into what each person wants it to be—an "iChurch." It is a group or a club to which we as individuals come a few times a week (but probably just once) to worship or learn individually and then go home as individuals to our individual lives. With this comes the attitude that what I do in my free time is my business, how I spend my money is my business, and my beliefs are my personal business. Church today has become yet another product of our culture's individualistic con-sumerist tendencies. We no longer understand what it means to be the church. The necessity of church fades away in the radiant market of free choice because we can read Scripture, pray, worship, and do missions on our own. Or so our culture tells us.

The Scriptures, however, offer a different story. Genesis gives us a vision of humans created in the image of God: a God who is a trinitarian God made up of three relationships, meaning that inherent within us is a need to be in relationship. The Gospels tell the story of Jesus praying in his final moments that his followers would all be one, in unity, together. The epistles speak of a community of worshipers filled with the Holy Spirit, who gather together to witness to the world that a different life is possible. Revelation speaks of the redemption of all creation, participat-ing together in the mission of God for the glory of God. As theologian Miroslav Volf explains, in the church we are gathered together as a con-gregation with the triune God and made a part of a history extending from the Old Testament through Christ to the new creation.[1] Scripture describes a people grafted into this story and made part of the people of God, where together in community we imitate the character of God and participate in God's mission of redeeming humanity and restoring God's peace to the world.

Church on the Way

Scholars point to several helpful images in the Scriptures to define and frame what it means to be the church in the world. Many see three primary images emerging from the New Testament: that of the people of God, the temple of the Holy Spirit, and the Body of Christ (although one scholar indicates there may be as many as ninety-six).[2] All of these images offer great insight and helpful paths for envisioning what it means be the church. The image of the people of God connects the New Testament congregation with its Hebrew roots, helping Christians understand ourselves as a continuation of the story of Israel, a grafting onto the covenant people of God. The image of the temple of the Holy Spirit frames the church as the place where God dwells and describes the church as the people God sends to the world to continue God's mission, empowered by God's Spirit.

For the purposes of this book, the image of the church as the Body of Christ is a vital framework for conceiving Christian identity. In this way, the church, local and universal, is an "extension of the incarnation" and the vehicle for Christ's continuing work of redemption and reconciliation.[3] This image also denotes a level of communalism and responsibility for the members of the church. The church is a unified Body where each member has a gift, each is a part of the Body, and each is responsible for one another (1 Cor 12:17; Rom 12:5; Eph 4). As a seminary friend once described, the individual is only a body part; the Body is what is primary. This image reinforces the primal nature of Christian community as existing before modern notions of autonomous individualism. In this way, I understand the image of the church as the Body of Christ to be more than metaphorical rhetoric. Appropriating a more literal consideration of the image, after Christ's ascension and since the Spirit's work at Pentecost, the church is Christ's actual presence *in* and *for* the world.

Theologians Karl Barth and Dietrich Bonhoeffer both employed a literal interpretation of this image in their work. "There is no need to take the statements symbolically or metaphorically," Barth claimed. "As His earthly-historical form of existence, the community is His body, His body is the community." In light of the event of Christ's death, resurrection, and gift of the Holy Spirit, Barth suggested the church community's earthly-historical existence can be understood as "the earthly-historical existence of Jesus Christ Himself."[4] The literalness of the image is even more profound and prominent in the ecclesiological works of Bonhoeffer. In fact, for Bonhoeffer, the church community was the present instantiation of Christ's incarnation: "Christ existing as church community."[5] Between Christ's ascension and return, the church is Christ's form in the world. Identifying the church as the Body of Christ, Bonhoeffer suggested, is more than symbolism. "The Church *is* the body of Christ," he claimed. "It does not *signify* the body."[6] While I will not explicate the deeper theology of this image here, the theme of the church as Christ's unified Body underlines the chapters of this book.

Another image often overlooked in academic and congregational literature, though explicit in Scripture, is that of the church as "the Way." While this image is not as prevalent as some others (occurring only in Acts), it appears that in founding their identity on Jesus' call to follow him, this was the name the early church gave itself. When referring to the groups of believers that had begun gathering in Jerusalem, Antioch, and elsewhere, Luke, the writer of Acts, often spoke of these men and women as belonging to "the Way." The name occurs in this context at least six times in Luke's narrative, twice from the mouth of Paul.[7] When Paul was finally captured at the temple in Jerusalem by a troop of Roman soldiers after the crowds began turning against him, he asked for a chance to address the crowd. He first admitted he was previously one who "persecuted this Way" by placing men and women in prison (22:4). Then before the Roman governor Felix at Caesarea, he confessed, "this I admit to you, that according to the Way, which they call a sect, I worship the God of our ancestors" (24:14). Paul identified himself with this designation and Body of believers. The church at this time was already considered a sect, a social counter to the Roman empire and Roman religious cults, and was called "the Way" by its followers.

This image, like the others discussed briefly above, maintains major implications for ecclesiology, that is, how Christians understand what it means to *be* the church.[8] This term in Greek, *hodos*, is one of the more frequently used words in the New Testament. In its literal usage, it refers to a road or a path, as in Saul was on the road (*hodos*) to Damascus when he had the odd encounter that forever changed his name. It is the same term Jesus used in his often misused confession in John 14:6 ("I am the Way, the Truth, and the Life"). And here, this term indicating some avenue for movement is given as the title of the church, the gathered community of believers. The church is not stationary. It is not a building. It is not even a location confined to a piece of property or spot on a metaphorical social map. Instead, the church is a path. It is a movement through time. It is a group of people on the move with an intended destination, a destiny not yet fully realized. Luke intended for his readers to understand the church as a gathered body of believers on a mission. In other words, the church is on a pilgrimage.

Theologians Stanley Hauerwas and Will Willimon, in their premier work on ecclesiology, supported this concept of the pilgrim church as they emphasized the image of the church as a colony on a journey. The church is in a constant state of anticipation, existing on the "long haul" in the chaotic times between one advent and the next.[9] It exists through its practices, such as Communion, that serve both as reminders of the past events and as anticipation of the future events of an eschatological community on the move, navigating through these "in-between times." Nigel Wright summed up this paradoxical existence by proclaiming that "the future defines us." The purpose of this pilgrimage—"what we are traveling towards"—is what forms our identity.[10] The identity of the church resides in its temporality, its mission, and its practices along the way. How we live, that is, our discipleship, emerges from this identity. In other words, we cannot be proper disciples unless we understand where we are going.

Most people could understand this image of the church as a colony of pilgrims on the move better in an oppressive country or under a regime that restricted religious liberty. However, you may be asking, why is this image needed in North America today? Does the church really need to view itself as a colony separate from the rest of the world when it finds itself in a country that is extremely amicable to its presence? While this image at first glance may seem unnecessary, I invite you to think about the American culture of materialism, sexual obsession, patriotism, privatized rights, and other influences fighting for Christians' allegiance while running counter to the vision of the church. The church is always on the margin of society, whether in a "restricted" country or in a nation of pluralism like the United States (and if it doesn't find itself in this position, you can bet that it is not doing something right.) It is always situated in opposition to empire. The early church opposed the Roman Empire and its obligatory allegiance and devotion to Caesar. Today's church in North America is no different. Rather than Caesar, today's church offers an alternative to the empire of materialism and sexualism and its temptation of wealth and instant pleasure, the empire of self-sufficiency and its myth of individual autonomy and independence, the empire of nationalism and its temptation of placing loyalty to country over loyalty to God. All of these "empires" maintain their own version of salvation—whether it is security in wealth, one's own abilities, social status, or national defense.

The church, however, has always been called to be a people "set apart," which is a continuation of God's calling to Israel to be a peculiar and holy people. In this vein, the church exists as a social alternative that doesn't make sense to those who do not worship Jesus as Lord. This does not mean that those in the church always act "set-apart" or that the church is never in need of repentance. The good news, rather, is that God's transformation of the world occurs through (and at times despite) the broken, sinful body of the church. Still in a culture in which Christians seem unclear about why their faith matters ethically, the church today would do well to remember, above all else, its "set apartness" and its pilgrim journey, and it does this through distinctive pilgrim practices.[11]

Just as pilgrims need specific practices to sustain and form them, a pilgrimage also cannot happen without commitment—not only commitment to see the journey through but commitment to join with others on the dangerous journey. This is a commitment to move beyond the iChurch mentality of church as a club, a rehab facility, or merely one personal commitment among many. The need for stronger commitment is why the idea of covenant, a central theme in the Scriptures describing God's relationship with God's people, is so essential for the community of disciples and so foundational to the church. God makes numerous covenants with God's people, from the Hebrews' escape from Egypt to Peter's declaration in Acts that believers are "heirs of the prophets and of the covenant" (Exod 6; Acts 3). The cup of Christ is described as a new covenant (1 Cor 11:25) joining the church not only to God through its remembrance and practice of Communion but also to each other in binding ways. In an article on the importance of local church covenants, Paul Fiddes quoted an early English Baptist leader, describing the founding of a local congregation. They "joyned themselves into a Church . . . to walke in all his ways."[12] This image of walking together is foundational to an understanding of discipleship. Church means a group of people covenanting to "walk together," that is, to pilgrimage.

Disciples on the Way

As you examine important sections of Scripture in this book, I hope your effort serves as a call to imagine what it means to be church, what it means to be a community of faith and mission, and how to reemploy important concepts such as discipleship. Often churches understand discipleship to be a program within the church. We have discipleship nights, discipleship studies, or discipleship classes, mistakenly confining this term to Christian education. It seems that recently there is a modest attempt at the retrieval of sufficient understandings of discipleship, but many in the pew are still confused and asking, "What do these words mean, and what do they have to do with me?" Looking to Scripture, we find a worthy answer in the book of James. There, the writer locates the meaning of discipleship within the church community—you cannot be a disciple by yourself. As Volf asserts, "No one can come to faith alone, and no one can live in faith alone . . . . It is in the church that one learns how faith is to be understood and lived."[13] It takes a community, and it takes a church.

The important thing to remember is this: discipleship is not an educational program or mission project. It is not a question of right doctrine or right behavior. Discipleship is fundamentally an issue of identity. Discipleship is the process of being formed through and by the church into part of the Body of Christ. *The Christian mission—the goal and the Way of discipleship—is essentially about the formation and transformation of identity.*[14]

Emmanuel Katongole, a Ugandan priest, tells the story of a visit to post-genocide Rwanda. The Hutu people had massacred 800,000 Tutsis in a matter of months in 1994, and the country was now in a period of much-needed reconciliation. As he was visiting a genocide site, he saw a Hutu woman spreading preservative on some of the dead bodies for the upcoming memorial. Seeing her move methodically, he asked her, "Where were you during the genocide?" "I was here," she responded. "Were you afraid?" he questioned again. "No," she replied. "I was not one of the ones to be killed."[15] Her casual, emotionless response demonstrated the power that the socially constructed identities of Hutu and Tutsi had on the people of Rwanda. This horrifying illustration demonstrates the power of identity, even imposed and false identities, upon us. The stories we tell ourselves and identities given to us often go unquestioned. It is simply the way things are.

This book, however, offers a different vision. From the perspective of Scripture, discipleship is about allowing pilgrim practices to reform our social, political, and economic identities. The images of Scripture tell a different story and offer a different image than the images of our world, suggesting that we are who we are because of the life, death, and resurrection of Christ. Christian identity is therefore not grounded in what people say, think, or feel. It is what we do. It is grounded in the particular, and peculiar, practices of the church.[16]

Finally, it is important to note the theological and missional connection between church and practices. The church, along with the identity of its members, is constituted by its practice. The church is embodied by the practices that make its Body visible in the world, that make its witness to the world distinctive. Through its practices, the church shares in the activity and mission of God to reconcile and redeem the world. In fact, it is through the practices of the church that the church exists as the one Body of Christ formed of different members. The church reflects the character of God and participates in and with God in God's mission. When we follow Christ as disciples, only then are we participating in God's mission and only then are we truly who we are meant to be, not an iChurch but *the* Church, where slowly, faithfully, and together, pilgrims can change the world.

3

Participating with God, or
The Original (Missional) Church

MOST OF THOSE WARY of the declining cultural relevance of church in North America today seek a solution through the concept of being "missional." There is much buzz revolving around this term in many denominational, congregational, and academic settings, so there is no need for me to explore the concept in depth.[1] Nearly any Christian conference offers courses or seminars on missional living, the missional journey, or being a "missional church." However, as is often the case with buzz terms, there is still much confusion about the meaning of the word. I will understand this word to mean the practice of participating with and in God in God's mission to reconcile and redeem the world. This definition finds its root in 2 Corinthians 5:17–21 where Paul describes Christians as "ambassadors for Christ." God makes God's appeal through us and gives us the "ministry of reconciliation." Missional essentially means our daily participation in the mission and ministry of the Triune God.

As much talk as there is about this concept, it seems odd in our present context that the term "missional" is often connected to the word "church." It is odd because there could not be a more redundant pair of words. The fact that we must use the term "missional church" to define a church that does God's work in the world demonstrates a great failure of the church. While the "missional church" has become one of the more popular marketing terms in church literature, a church being "missional" is not a new concept. In fact, it is one of the oldest concepts in Christianity, and is not an option for Christians—not something churches or individuals can choose. It is who we are to begin with. The church is not something that is or is not missional. The very nature and meaning of the church is missional—to be a community that brings glory to God by living as the instrument of God's mission on the earth. Being missional is, in effect, being the church. In this way, the church points to both the future coming and the current presence of the kingdom of God on earth. Gaining traction in recent years, the "missional" concept is by no means new. While he did not use the term, the seminal theologian Karl Barth emphasized this notion of participating in God's mission. Writing more than fifty years ago, Barth asserted that humanity is caught up in a "dynamic movement of the Creator to itself and itself to the Creator."[2] In fact, humanity participates in the continuing history of Jesus and lives with God as God's "covenant-partner." As covenant-partner, we participate in history in which God is at work with us and we with God.[3] While Barth's language of partnership preceded contemporary missional language, we could go back even further to uncover a more basic description of the missional church—nearly 2,000 years earlier.

Beginning at the Beginning

There is no need to move any further than the New Testament description of the original church to find a biblical description of what it means to be a "missional" church—or simply a church. Examining the church through the lens of Acts 2 will serve to cast the scene for my exploration of specific pilgrim practices in the second part of this book. The book of Acts is a fitting starting point for a work on communal discipleship framed by the book of James because of the connection between these two books of Scripture.

Traditionally scholars have believed the author of the letter of James to be the brother of Jesus, the leader of the first church in Jerusalem—that is, the James described in Acts 15 and 21. In this case, the writer of this letter would be the leader of the congregation described in Acts 2 and 4.[4] While this of course cannot be incontrovertibly proven, it is certain that the writer of the book had considerable contact with early congregations .

in the Palestinian area and knew deeply the struggles of the church. It is not a far stretch to assume that the writer of James had contact and knew quite well the story of Pentecost and the ensuing gathered community described in Acts 2 and 4.

If the writer is the James of Acts, he enters the story in Acts 15 when he is called to deliberate among questions concerning Gentile adherence to Jewish law. Peter, Paul, and Barnabas advocate for Gentile inclusion without the Jewish law in response to certain teachers in Antioch and Pharisee representatives (Acts 15:1–5). James speaks with authority for the apostles and points to the importance of unity for the early Christians. In this way, the James described in Acts, who witnessed the sacrificial economic, political, and social unity of the early church, provides an "angle of vision toward the letter of James."[5] In other words, the events of Acts and the grand unity of the church described here certainly affect the focus and themes of James's letter. He echoes perhaps the most significant theme in the entire letter and foreshadows the missional and communal perspective of this book on discipleship: the unity of the church. James's ecclesiological focus frames his entire letter and situates discipleship within the life and practice of the community of faith. With this connection in mind, it is easier to understand why the ecclesial description in Acts 2:42–47 helps to situate James's focus and the church practices espoused in his letter.

Luke begins in Acts 2,

> They devoted themselves to the apostles' teaching and fellowship, to the breaking of bread and the prayers. Awe came upon everyone, because many wonders and signs were being done by the apostles. All who believed were together and had all things in common; they would sell their possessions and goods and distribute the proceeds to all, as any had need. Day by day, as they spent much time together in the temple, they broke bread at home and ate their food with glad and generous hearts, praising God and having the goodwill of all the people. And day by day the Lord added to their number those who were being saved. (Acts 2:42–47)

Teaching, fellowship, breaking bread, prayer, having all things in common, sharing with all who had need, adding to their number, and praising God. These practices defined the life of the early church as a missional community and distinguished Christian life from the regular patterns of the world. Behaving and living in patterns far removed from traditional

Roman ways of life, where Roman authorities demanded emperor worship, social stratification, and national military service, these early disciples existed as an alternative society living as strangers and pilgrims in the empire. This small community of believers was unbreakably linked to the mission and work of God in the world. They understood themselves as the Body of Christ, carrying on the work of Jesus in "foreign" territory—the truest sense of "missional" I can imagine. One scholar of the missional movement, Alan Roxburgh, describes the idea in this way: "Missional Church is about a people of memory being continually formed in practices that shape us as an alternative story in our culture."[6] These practices form the church into what Roxburgh calls a contrast society—which is a great image for understanding the distinctiveness of discipleship. A contrast society is a people shaped by an alternative story and living by a set of distinctly Christian practices,[7] as this depiction of the early church in the midst of the Roman Empire demonstrates.

To understand this passage fully, one also cannot overlook the events just prior to Luke's ecclesiological description in Acts 2. As people from all over the world gathered in Jerusalem, and Peter was preparing to deliver a sermon, suddenly the Holy Spirit came down upon the disciples and those around them began hearing them speak in their own languages. The gospel transcended language, ethnicity, and geography that day. Pentecost—the birthday of the church. The church was instituted with people from every nation, together, worshiping as one. This shared experience created a notion of community beyond ethnic boundaries, beyond social hierarchies, and beyond cultural traditions, and became the basis for the vision of church that we see in Luke's description.

Tutu and Ubuntu

In a 2007 edition of *Vanity Fair* (perhaps not the magazine in which you would expect to find solid theology), Brad Pitt interviewed Archbishop Desmond Tutu of South Africa. After leading South Africa through its struggle against Apartheid and then through the Truth and Reconciliation Commission, Tutu, world-renowned and Nobel Prize-winning leader for peace, spoke about the South African concept of *ubuntu*. In the article he explained to Pitt, "*Ubuntu* is the essence of being human. In our language *ubuntu* is a noun to speak about what it means to be a person. We say a person is a person through other persons. We say, 'I need you to be all of who you are in order for me to be all that I am.' You can't be a human in isolation. You are a person only in relationships."[8] This South African concept is, in fact, not far from the biblical vision of church. As Christians, we understand that God created us for relationships. God created the church to be not a group of individuals but a community that is stronger because people are together. As a pastor friend once told me, there are two things you can never be by yourself—married and a Christian!

For the early church, this idea of fellowship was central. When I think of fellowship, my mind automatically jumps to food. My thoughts drift to mouth-watering images of potluck lunches with chicken pie and baked spaghetti, essential vegetables like squash casserole and macaroni and cheese, along with all the desserts I could dream of. While this image is close to the important practice of eating together in the early church, the idea of fellowship means so much more. Luke uses the Greek term *koinonia*, which we translate as "fellowship." For the early church, *koinonia* was more than potluck meals. It was more than occasional gatherings or trips to a baseball game. Similar to Tutu's understanding of *ubuntu*, it was a way of living. *Koinonia* in ancient Greek was a term used to describe the most intimate relationships. It referred to the union of marriage and even to the fellowship of the Trinity, the intimate closeness of Father, Son, and Holy Spirit. It did not imply passive association. *Koinonia* is an active fellowship that requires participation. Within the local church, Christians participate in a close bond, in a relationship as close as marriage, as close as the Trinity. In fact, you could say Christians participate along with God in this Trinitarian relationship reaching out together as God's hands and feet to the world—the missional life.[9] Being missional is being drawn up into the life, relationships, and work of God; it is participating *in* God.

This, however, is where many writers on missional church or Christian practices can be misleading. Many times, people speak of fellowship or community as one practice among the others, placing the action of engaging in community in the same vein as prayer or charity. It is important to understand that, as an alternative to the individualized Christianity we have come to know and live, community is not itself one of the practices in which individual members are called to participate. Rather, "community is the context in which all the practices take place."[10]

Come to the Table

This *koinonia* was expressed through the breaking of bread. Often when we read this, we think of Communion, the Lord's Supper. The church in Acts, however, did not have tiny clear cups of grape juice and little pieces of crunchy crackers like many congregations today. I remember looking forward to Communion Sundays as a child for the completely irreverent reason that I loved grape juice. But for these early believers, breaking bread involved a full meal shared together. It was not only a time of remembrance of Christ's sacrifice but also a time to enjoy fellowship and share with the entire community. The meal represented Jesus' death and indicated the social, economic, and political barriers that he came to break down.

In the ancient world, mealtime was an opportunity to reinforce cultural hierarchies. As Jesus indicates in one of his parables, where you sat at mealtime was determined by your social status (Luke 14:7-10). When I was growing up, at all our big family meals, like Thanksgiving and Christmas, we had an adult table and a kid table. I looked forward to the day I could move up from the child table to the adult one. To me, it was a rite of passage, an honor. As great as it seemed in my mind to sit at the adult table, I remember my aunt always coming and sitting with us at the kid table. She forsook her place of "honor" and came to the lowly place where the kids ate. She broke down any social distinctions in our family, and that is exactly what the church meals represented. Through the breaking of bread, sharing together without hierarchy, the church broke down the intense social barriers of their culture and even their religion. Everyone was welcomed, no matter how much money you made, no matter how powerful or influential you were, no matter what you did for a living, no matter what you did last night. Food was shared with everyone equally as a small sign of the kingdom. As Yoder noted, sharing the bread and cup is a matter of economic ethics.[11] The church saw no distinction between the spiritual and social dimensions of the meal. For us just as for the early church, the bread and wine binds believers not only to God but also to one another, cultivating a social posture that is open to sharing with all as they have need. "The one bread that is given to our fellowship links us together in a firm covenant," wrote Bonhoeffer. "None dares go hungry as long as another has bread, and he who breaks this fellowship of the physical life also breaks the fellowship of the Spirit."[12]

That They May All Be One

"All the believers had all things in common." The church opened its doors and shared food with anyone, and they also sold their possessions and property and divided the proceeds among everyone, sharing with people in need. The outpouring of the Holy Spirit at Pentecost led these early believers to share everything they had with whomever had need. A popular study reveals that only one out of every eight regular church attendees gives at least 10 percent of his or her income annually.[13] Imagine a community of people offering everything each of them had, saying, "Give me back only what I need to live on and share the rest with everyone else." Most pastors would faint right on the spot! But that is the social agenda represented here. God called this community to live differently as a contrast society, to live according to a different set of values and patterns of living, not according to the pattern of this world. For them, wealth and status lost all value. For them, no person created in the image of God deserved to go hungry, go without clothes, or go without a place to stay. They divided their possessions evenly among the members of the community and reached out to help their neighbors who were in need.

The community that shared their possessions shared their passion for God as well. Verse 46 says they continued with one mind in the temple. It is interesting to note that they continued to meet in the Jewish temple. This group did not forget where they came from. I remember times when I complained growing up, and my mother would often respond by saying things like, "Back where I was from . . ." or "Back when I was growing up, I had to do . . . ," and then she would insert some absurd task like walking to school "uphill both ways." While I still question the historical accuracy of such statements, the message is vital. We are formed and shaped by where we come from. We are functions of how we imagine ourselves, suggested Katongole, and that is deeply connected to the stories we tell ourselves.[14] Our past experiences mold us into who we are today. These believers were molded by the Jewish temple, the rituals, and their identity with God into a group with "one mind." Even though Jesus had changed their understanding of God, they did not neglect their traditions.

Our church traditions shape us in the same way today. While the church has fallen many times throughout its history, the past 2,000 years have also brought us rituals, stories, and practices to form and shape us into better followers of Jesus—practices of prayer, ancient creeds, confession, almsgiving, nonviolence, and testimonies of faith. It is important for us not to neglect our traditions but to combine them with our new advances and understandings to move beyond our failures and become the kind of people who do good in the world—to become the kind of people who try to live as disciples.

The Unity of Commuity

This description of the early church is a vision of people living in the kingdom of God on earth. No one was hungry, no one was excluded, no one was alone, no one was in need. In our highly individualized "iSociety," it is hard for us to imagine living in such a way—a way where we share all we have so no one goes without, where we break down social hierarchies and ethnic barriers, where we remember our Savior and Lord every day as we gather and as we eat, where we try to be the type of community God would have God's church to be.

After reading this passage and this chapter, you may think, "This ancient church is some idyllic vision, if not a description of socialist propaganda or a hippie commune in the '70s. The whole church seems so sectarian, separated from the outside, real world. What good could a secluded community like this have done?" You may also suggest that this would never happen in America today. I must admit, you are right. If you look ahead to Paul's letters, some written less than fifteen years after the initiation of the communities described in Acts, you see that these communal ideas of sharing and these visions of being of one mind did not last long. Just open a few of Paul's letters to these churches and you will see that conflict, immoral behavior, and disputes crept in and tore churches apart.

It would be a wonderful ending to this story if the church existed in this form for 2,000 years. However, history reveals that it did not. Rather than continuing with one mind, the church split into thousands of denominations. Rather than caring for its members and reaching out to help those in need, the church has become so integrated with the political, economic, and social structures of society and so complicit with positions of power that it tends to neglect those less fortunate while increasing its own power. Rather than adding to its numbers, the church has seen the percentage of Americans *not* attending services nearly double in the past fifteen years.

While theorists identify numerous reasons for this, the point is that regardless of the "practicality" of this vision, right now we as the church are not doing our job. We are not fulfilling our calling. We are not acting like a community of disciples. We are not living as a pilgrim people on God's mission.

People today are searching for meaning in their lives. They are searching for people who care—and not just about them but about important issues and struggles in our world: people who care about conflict in Palestine and war in Iraq, the twelve million AIDS orphans in Africa, and the hungry children in the house down the street. They are searching for a place to belong, for a community that offers something greater than we are on our own as individuals.

And the church is falling short.

I believe the biggest reason this vision of the church does not make sense to us as modernized, western Christians is because we read it so individually. It does not make sense for me to give up all my possessions— I'm not sure I have the faith that I would still be taken care of by others. The problem is that we are trained to view life individually and not through communal lenses. The vision here in Acts is that everyone in this small community would share their wealth and care for those who have none, care for those who can no longer work, care for those who are different from them, care for those who continually mess up, care for those who cannot get their lives together. It is a community whose members live more humbly so they may bless the world. That is true *ubuntu*. That is *koinonia*.

People may read this story in Acts and think of it only as a *description* of the early church. But perhaps—even though this church was located halfway around the world 2,000 years ago in a completely foreign context—this is also a *prescription* for us. I'm not asking you to sell everything you own and take all the proceeds to share with everyone at your church (at least not this early in the book—I want you to continue reading!). Perhaps, however, Luke's vision of community, of people gathering together to share the joy of life, remember the life of Jesus, and embody the Body of Christ for those in need, should form us into a similar community. Perhaps we should be the type of community that offers a place to belong, a vision of care, a people on a journey, a mission to save the world. A community, a *koinonia*.[15]

God has a mission for us. God wants us to be the type of community that people look at and say, "They are different. They are up to something, and I want to be a part of that." Jesus says the kingdom of God starts like a mustard seed, but that the seed can turn into a great bush and make a great impact. At the end of Acts 2, Luke says the Lord added to their number daily. It is important to note that Luke says the *Lord* added. It was not the work of individuals, but it was simply the job of the church to have the faith to let God work through them.

Looking Ahead

Thus far I have attempted to "cast the scene" for a beneficial discussion of pilgrim practices. Hopefully the discussion so far has shed new (and old) light on the concepts of pilgrimage, practice, community, and, most important, discipleship. Part II moves through the book of James, examining specific communal practices James envisioned for the churches, practices that form the body of believers into pilgrims who are woven together into the Body of Christ. Before turning to the first practice, allow me to offer some background for the book of James.

Most scholars agree that this letter was written to the first generation of Christians scattered throughout the Mediterranean region—the "dispersion." James had a bird's-eye view of the early church. He saw its strengths and its shortcomings, and most of its shortcomings were ethical. The church was struggling to be good disciples—"servant[s] of God and the Lord Jesus Christ" (Jas 1:1).

James wrote not to one particular church but offered a general letter—in fact, somewhat of a sermon—to be distributed to all churches throughout the region. Unlike some other New Testament texts, James was written to people who were already Christian or were at least familiar with this curious practice and faith. It is an ethical document explaining how to join God's mission in the world and live into this new identity of "Christian"—how to live in the kingdom of God.

It is a letter both *from* and *for* the church, which is why it serves so appropriately as a basis for our task of better understanding communal discipleship. James offers a vivid and articulate vision of discipleship unlike any other in the Scriptures. Of course, the story of Israel, the Gospel narratives of Jesus, and the church imagery of Paul all move us along in a path of discipleship, and the book of James incorporates the major themes from all these sources and weaves them together into a clear call to community as the path for discipleship. While the church today spends so much time on discipleship programs, James rightly discerned that being a disciple is an identity entailing a lifestyle of mission and a lifestyle in community with other Christians.

In five dense chapters, James explains what it means to be the church. This book, more than any other outside the Gospels, parallels the teachings of Jesus—especially his Sermon on the Mount. It serves as a bold reminder that our Christian faith matters for how we live our lives. Discipleship is not only about believing the correct things but also, perhaps even more so, about living the right way. Discipleship is about living faithfully and missionally through the church community. This is not to say James is a perfect, comprehensive document; one could point out certain areas of practice where James is lacking. For example, I personally wish there were more explicit references to the formative roles of baptism, Communion, and the significance of the Trinity. These themes, however, implicitly underline most of James's social ethic. In the end, the book of James serves as a much-needed call to discipleship for the missional community of God.

Based on the themes in James's letter, this book is an invitation to communal practices of discipleship—pilgrim practices—knowing that we can never do alone what we can do for and with God as part of a church. The prophetic voice of James goes beyond the popular contemporary invocation of living "missionally," compelling us to be a missional community in and through the local church. Only together, as a church, can we live in a way that witnesses to the principalities and powers of this world and blesses the world though God's mission.

PART II

Eight Pilgrim Practices

4

Believing: Faith Beyond Limits

JAMES, A SERVANT OF *God and of the Lord Jesus Christ, to the twelve tribes in the Dispersion:*

Greetings. My brothers and sisters, whenever you face trials of any kind, consider it nothing but joy, because you know that the testing of your faith produces endurance; and let endurance have its full effect, so that you may be mature and complete, lacking in nothing.

If any of you is lacking in wisdom, ask God, who gives to all generously and ungrudgingly, and it will be given you. But ask in faith, never doubting, for the one who doubts is like a wave of the sea, driven and tossed by the wind; for the doubter, being double-minded and unstable in every way, must not expect to receive anything from the Lord. (James 1:1–8)

"Unstable." "Like a wave." "Driven and tossed." These words are important images with which to begin this journey into deepening discipleship. These images remind me of times when I've been at the ocean or on the lake during a storm. I remember watching the waves in the Atlantic days before an approaching hurricane. Waves that softly drifted ashore just days earlier were now crashing violently into the sandy beach, the grey water swirling behind them. These images also remind me of white-water rafting. The small raft flailing around violently amid sharp rocks, blustery canyons, and rapid swells of water left me feeling literally unstable as I was driven and tossed by the wind and water.

The New Testament writer James uses these images in James 1 to describe a person who doubts, who has a life without purpose, commitment, and faith. For James, this is not a person who occasionally questions his or her faith or a person who sometimes wonders if God is really here. With this term, James identifies a person who does not believe—a person removed from faith in God.[1] He contends that these "doubters" are tossed around like waves in the sea or perhaps, in a modern analogy, like rafters on a raging river. Vulnerable, continuously up and down, pushed, pulled, and scattered in different directions. In a sermon-letter filled with many captivating images, James begins with a depiction of lost faith. In the first eight verses of his letter, three prominent themes emerge—trials, wisdom, and faith—and in the space of a few sentences James weaves these seemingly unrelated concepts into a grand vision of discipleship for the community of God.

An Unusual Beginning

This first chapter of James serves as an introduction to the rest of his letter, introducing the foundational themes he will expand later. His opening greeting to the churches contains none of the typical missive formalities—no thanksgiving for his readers, no praise hymn to God, no prayer for evangelistic growth. He writes rather informally, in a sermonic and even conversational tone. It seems that James knows his intended readers well.[2] Unlike many of us preachers, speakers, or writers today, James gets straight to the point. A person with no faith is like a wave—tossed around, unstable, lost at sea with no place to belong.

At this point you may be wondering, if James is a book primarily concerned with ethical living, concentrating on the "works" of discipleship as opposed to the centrality of faith, isn't it odd that he begins with the concept of faith? The book of James was nearly left out of the biblical canon for its lack of emphasis on faith, but here in the introduction to the book, James asserts that believing is essential to the Christian life.

On a personal level, I struggle with beginning a lesson on discipleship with belief. I believe that for too long Protestant churches have focused on correct doctrine at the expense of right practice—orthodoxy over orthopraxy—to the detriment of Jesus' social calling in the gospel. In the process of discipleship, and even that of conversion, I believe true faith can and often does begin after true practice. (If one begins acting like a Christian, sooner or later she or he will begin to believe like a Christian!) But James chooses to begin by highlighting faith. Echoing statements elsewhere in the New Testament, he asserts that without faith nothing is possible. God is good and desires to give God's people tremendous gifts, and this we must believe. Without belief we are tossed about in the chaotic, choppy sea of life.

The question remains, however, as to why James places such a primary stress on belief. The clue comes in verses 2–4. James's readers are facing trials and persecution. They are tempted to rely on their own strength—to guide themselves through the treacherous "white water." But James asserts that trust in God is the key to facing trials; the path of discipleship begins with faith.

You may also think it is odd to claim belief as a distinct pilgrim practice. Many pastors, theologians, and writers often separate belief and practice in the Christian life, but James attempts to connect them throughout this book (find more on this subject in chapter 7, "Committing"). For James, belief is a Christian practice—it is a habit developed and cultivated over time. Faith does not derive from evidence; we cannot prove the resurrection happened, that God created the world out of nothing, or that a man who walked the shores of Galilee 2,000 years ago was in fact God-with-us. These are things Christians choose to believe for many different reasons, but mostly because God calls us to this belief, and as James later asserts, God even "implants" this great Word within us. Yet it is still a faith we must work toward, work out, and develop through the ups and downs of life. Frederick Buechner, in his work *The Return of Ansel Gibbs*, said,

> Every morning you should wake up in your beds and ask yourself: "Can I believe it all again today?" No, better still, don't ask it until after you've read *The New York Times*, till after you've studied that daily record of the world's brokenness and corruption . . . . Then ask yourself if you can believe in the Gospel of Jesus Christ again that particular day. If your answer's always Yes, then you probably don't know what believing means.[3]

Believing is a practice we must constantly engage, struggle with, and allow to form us as we travel on this pilgrimage of discipleship. Temporary questions and doubts are bound to creep in. It is not always simple or easy, but faith is a commitment that entails continuous renewal.

The Wisdom of Trials

"Whenever you face trials of any kind, consider it nothing but joy," James suggests. Any modern psychologist would lose her job with such outlandish statements. Tell this to the earthquake victim who has lost everything. Tell it to the couple who has lost a child. Tell the patient who is diagnosed with AIDS to consider it only joy. How on earth could such unrealistic words come from a Scripture that we consider sacred? With the multitude of contemporary voices that offer images of being tested by a wrathful God who must punish or cause suffering on earth in order to teach a lesson, we rightly read such passages with extreme caution. In his outrageous assertion, James is not suggesting causation from God, but explaining to his readers that, though God may not cause suffering to happen, we should endure the cause of the pain as a test. He does not say why trials come and why people suffer but only hopes that they grow from trials when they do come. For his persecuted readers in the first century, this was a radical understanding of trials. Trials are not punishment for past sins or a consequence of divine wrath; rather, regardless of cause, they are occasions to grow—even to grow in wisdom.

James quickly moves from endurance in trials to the theme of wisdom. He says growing through trials will make disciples mature and complete. This completeness, it seems, is manifest in wisdom. Wisdom will be an important theme throughout James's letter—it is imperative for living a life of discipleship. Here, he places wisdom directly after a discussion on suffering in order to indicate that wisdom can help Christians better understand trials (and perhaps trials can help make us wiser). While we may never know why we suffer, with wisdom we can better know what to glean from difficult circumstances. Endurance in trials brings about wisdom, and wisdom, in turn, helps us to endure and grow mature in discipleship through trials.

And the key is that all we have to do is ask! James describes God as a merciful and generous giver of gifts to all humanity—not the least of which is wisdom. A true disciple asks God, depends on God, and also trusts God to follow through with God's promises. This leads to James's final theme in this section: faith.

The Practice of Faith

When James, in verse 6, tells his readers to "ask in faith," he uses the Greek word *pistis*. This word is used throughout the New Testament in many prominent verses like John 3:16—the noun form for *faith*, the verb form for *believe*. In fact, it is one of the most important words in all of Scripture. The true impact of this important term *pistis* cannot be captured in a one- or two-word translation. It means much more than typical definitions of the word "faith"; it means to entrust yourself completely to something or someone, to have so much faith that you rely on them. It is not just belief; it is a complete and trusting commitment.[4] It is being committed to the ultimate notion that God *is* good.

Pistis moves beyond intellectual assent or even an acknowledgment that something is true. Believing in the biblical sense means participating in that truth; it means being a part of God's truth, work, and mission. Belief is not passive. By its very definition, it is active and missional; it means being on the Way. For James, it seems that a person must have wisdom in order to grow in faith and must have faith in God to provide that wisdom. A person who doubts God, who does not believe, is lost in a stormy sea—like the disciples on the boat in Galilee, waiting for Jesus and frightened in the storm (Matt 14:22–33; Mark 6:45–51; John 6:15–21); like Peter taking his eyes off Jesus and sinking into the waves. Tossed, unstable, double-minded—that is, trusting in God but always having a "back-up plan." Believing in God but considering other options, just in case. Placing faith in God but also granting allegiance to other authorities—national powers, economics, science, or technology. Karl Barth articulated James's thought, saying this double-minded person "may think that he should and can live dualistically, in the twin kingdoms of public and private life. He lives in the knowledge of faith, but he is prepared to live this obedient faith only within certain limits." Barth concluded by saying, "When he half believes, he cannot expect to know any more than half."[5] Faith "within certain limits" is one of the sturdiest barriers to a life of discipleship.

For many, faith "beyond limits" is one of the most difficult practices of the Christian pilgrimage. I know that I often fall into the trap of "half-believing" and thinking I can take care of things myself. Most Americans are trained to be independent from the time we are young, and it goes against everything we are taught to rely fully on someone else—even if that someone is God.

Discussions of faith and trust in God always take me back to the search for my first full-time ministry position after seminary. During one of the most stressful periods of my life, I became more and more discouraged as graduation approached and I did not have a job. With every rejection letter my heart sank. I posted the first letter on my refrigerator as motivation to search more diligently, but as more rejections came, my humor and confidence faded. I even received rejection letters from churches to which I did not apply! As graduation passed, I began to question my calling as a minister and wondered where God was in all of this. If God was not going to do anything about it, I reasoned that I must rely on myself. I attempted to fix my own problems and look for ways out of such difficult circumstances on my own. It is often when situations start to go south that my prayer life is the worst, as I hunker down in doubt and pity and look for ways to lift myself out. Despite many preconceived notions, even ministers struggle with faith and full dependence on God.

I remember a time as a child at church camp when I attempted to walk across a waste area—I called it "quicksand"—to prove my bravery to a few friends. As I achieved the halfway point and turned to gloat to my buddies, I suddenly sank to my thighs in the dark, suffocating mud. I panicked and immediately began squirming, trying to pull myself out of the miry soil. The more I tried to pull myself out of the situation, the worse it became and the deeper I sank. Often when we find ourselves in trials, we tend to forsake others—God, neighbors, friends, Christian family—and rely on ourselves. As we try to pull ourselves out of our difficult situations, we only sink deeper into them. Self-reliance is our solution to faith with limits, and often as trials continue to plague us and the future is uncertain, we struggle even to "half-believe."

It is difficult for pilgrims to understand that faith will not keep us from trials; they will still come. Faith, however, can help us to mature when trials enter our lives. It is also important to remember that James is writing to church communities and not individuals, so endurance through trials is not a divine test of the individual—as in the story of Abraham and Isaac (Gen 22)—but points to the faith of the entire community. The individual Christian is never expected to handle difficult circumstances on her or his own. In short, trusting God must be a communal practice. We must lift each other up when the doubts threaten to weigh us down.

Reality Check

At the outset of his letter, James is in a sense offering an alternative view of reality. He delivers a different understanding of trials and suffering—and a person needs faith in order to believe this reality. Here he lays the groundwork for what it means to be a pilgrim. Discipleship, beginning in faith, opens the door to a radically new understanding of reality, even a brand-new existence.[6]

In this new reality, God is the giver of all gifts. This is not a world filled with competition and violence but a place and a time for giving, just as God gives to us. It is a revolutionary belief and trust where we fully depend on God, through the church, not to avoid all struggles but to work through them and grow together in them. We no longer rely on ourselves for rescue out of miry circumstances and the pains of life but place our dependence on God through faith and on God's church. The priest and spiritual writer Henri Nouwen submitted, "A Christian community is therefore a healing community not because wounds are cured and pains are alleviated, but because wounds and pains become openings or occasions for a new vision."[7] As people living in the radical, missional community known as the church, this is the groundwork for what it means to be a disciple, transcending wounds and suffering and then transforming these pains into opportunities for a fresh vision.

The first step to discipleship, James offers, is believing in an alternative reality; believing that all we can see is not all there is. As Americans, we are formed by certain assumptions about ourselves, society, and politics. The stories that formed the founding of our society as a capitalist democracy are stories grounded in theories about competition, self-interest, and limited resources. From influential political theorists like Thomas Hobbes we have been formed to believe that reality must entail individual "social contracts" of nation-states to secure us from a primordial state of war. We must entrust sovereign governments to secure individual rights and protect us and our resources from others who would try to violate us. But James tells us that as disciples, we have a new Way and we can see a new reality—believing that the competition for resources, suffering, and violence of this world are not in control and do not have the final say. We trust in a different wisdom than the wisdom of the world. We do not exist merely as atomized, isolated individuals in need of violent protection and retributive justice. A state of war does not have to be the default state of existence, and nation-states do not have ultimate authority over morality. God wants to give us good gifts, the first of which is a new way to see the world—and that begins with faith. In 2 Corinthians, Paul says joining Christ creates not a new person, as we tend to think, but a new *world*: "If one is in Christ, there is a new world [or new creation]. The old order has gone and a new world has begun!"[8] We see faith not only as transformative for the individual believer, but as transforming the entire world through the mission and vision God grants to the church.

One of my favorite television series is the show *House, M.D.*, about an ornery, drug-addicted, yet genius medical doctor who diagnoses patients that no other doctor is able to diagnose. In one episode, he is treating a patient with a brain tumor that has deformed her vision since birth. While thinking she has always seen the world correctly, she has actually seen it as a dull, ugly place, without knowing that reality is actually much brighter. After her surgery, Dr. House stops by to check on her and says, "The world *is* an ugly place. People kill, people go hungry, people are asses. But the world isn't as ugly as you think it is." He explains to her that her brain has not been functioning properly and the tumor prevented it from correctly processing visual data. "You could see, but not see," he explains. "It was dull, foggy, or grey—I don't know which. What I do know is that you were not seeing what you could be seeing." As he begins to take off the gauze that cover her eyes, she asks, "So now things will be beautiful?" and he responds, "Things will be what they really are."

In the end, the practice of believing turns out to be the perfect place to begin a discussion of pilgrim practices. Without a framework of a particular form of faith—that of believing in God's goodness, believing in Christ as Lord, believing in the church's participation in God's mission, and believing in a brand-new reality that we can only see when we believe these other aspects of faith—a practice is no *pilgrim* practice at all. The pilgrim path of discipleship begins with the toughest step, believing—practicing trust in God even when our heads tell us not to, practic-ing trust even when it seems prudent to have a back-up plan, practicing trust when it does not make much sense in the reality we see all around us. It means having a faith beyond limitations, beyond mere intellectual assent, beyond half-beliefs. A life of drifting at sea, driven and tossed by the waves of doubt, is no life at all. In order to live missionally, in order to take the next step farther than we have ever been before, in order to join God's movement to reconcile, redeem, and bring the world back to God, God says we must first believe and see the beauty; we must see how things really are.

5

Listening: I Never Forget My Face

EVERY GENEROUS ACT OF giving, with every perfect gift, is from above, coming down from the Father of lights, with whom there is no variation or shadow due to change. In fulfillment of his own purpose he gave us birth by the word of truth, so that we would become a kind of first fruits of his creatures. You must understand this, my beloved: let everyone be quick to listen, slow to speak, slow to anger; for your anger does not produce God's righteousness.

Therefore rid yourselves of all sordidness and rank growth of wickedness, and welcome with meekness the implanted word that has the power to save your souls. But be doers of the word, and not merely hearers who deceive themselves. For if any are hearers of the word and not doers, they are like those who look at themselves in a mirror; for they look at themselves and, on going away, immediately forget what they were like. But those who look into the perfect law, the law of liberty, and persevere, being not hearers who forget but doers who act—they will be blessed in their doing. (James 1:17-25)

My mom and my sister have birthdays one day apart, July 20 and 21. I remember vividly a phone call from my mom that came late one summer afternoon. After the initial warm greetings, she gently questioned whether

I had been unusually busy or stressed, and whether I had forgotten anything important. Thinking for a second about her rather odd question, I glanced over at a calendar and realized what day it was. I knew instantly that I had completely forgotten my mother's and my sister's birthdays!

I had sent no presents. I had not called to sing "Happy Birthday." I had not even sent a card. I had completely forgotten.

Now you may be wondering what kind of no-good son could forget his family's birthdays, and believe me, I will always remember the utter embarrassment and disappointment of my memory lapse—my mother and sister will surely see to that! As human beings, however, we all have a tendency to be forgetful. We can stay up all night preparing for a presentation at work or preparing for an exam at school, but when it is time to begin, it is easy to forget the important details. We can tell ourselves that we will call a friend who is going through a rough time, but sometimes it slips our distracted minds. We can look out the window and see that the grass is getting higher and know we need to mow the lawn, but when the football game comes on, we might make ourselves forget! We can hear God urge us to take a chance, speak to a certain person, or to join a local church, but when it comes time to take action, it's simply convenient to forget. We hear, but we allow the words to go proverbially in one ear and out the other.

It is a lot easier to hear than it is to take action. It is easy to hear the word, but it is hard to be doers of the word. In this chapter's focal text from James 1, James says that hearing the word and not doing what it says is like a person looking in a mirror and then immediately forgetting what her or his face looks like.

But what does that mean? It seems silly. Couldn't James have come up with a more practical image? How is not doing what the word says like forgetting your own face?

First Fruits

After opening with an emphasis on faith as the starting point for discipleship, James begins this section with the theme of God's good gifts. This idea establishes a base for his entire letter and a foundation for the lives of his readers. God is gracious and wants to offer God's people good gifts. These gifts are meant to transform us and mold us into communities that embody and exhibit these gifts and live in ways different from the world. The world around us often lives according to an ethic of competition, selfishness, greed, and violence, but as the church, the Body of Christ, we live according to God's good gifts where we share so that no one has to go without, where we put others first, and where we know a different reality is possible. We are to live as a people transformed. We are to be "first fruits" of creation, as James says in verse 18, meaning we are to be a witness to these good gifts.

In the book of Deuteronomy, when the Israelites entered Canaan they offered the first fruits of their harvest to God. As he does several times in the letter, James references the Hebrew Scriptures, comparing us as Christians to an offering for God.[1] (In Romans 12, Paul similarly claims that we are to live our lives as "living sacrifices" to God.) Our lives are offerings to be dedicated to God, and this, of course, has major implications for discipleship.

Learning to Listen

The first way we live our lives as offerings to God is by listening and being slow to anger, James suggests (1:19). For James, listening is more than hearing. It is hearing in a way that effects a change in the listener. It involves action—hearing *and* doing. In other words, listening is transformative. The churches to which James wrote, like many today, were wracked by conflict. Disruptions and arguments were splitting them apart. They were being quick to anger and slow to give each other a chance or offer a listening ear. In our world, we are taught to speak first and speak loudest. That is how we get what we want. If we can just get our point across, if we can just make sure we look better or smarter than anyone else, we will win. If we just make sure everyone else knows how dumb they sound or how wrong they are, we will be proven right. But these ways do not approach the righteousness of God. Dietrich Bonhoeffer writes in his book *Life Together,* "The first service one owes to others in the community involves listening to them. Just as our love for God begins with listening to God's word, the beginning of love for other Christians is learning to listen to them."[2] And often this is the most difficult thing to do. Listening is the first step to peace. It is the first step to reconciliation. It is the first step to unity.

If we want to be communities that seek diversity, peace, and unity, we have to be people who listen to the whisper of God, who listen to the father who has just lost his job, who listen to the never-ending questions of a child, who listen to the disgruntled person who only wants to argue, who listen to the wife whose husband has terminal cancer. The practice of listening, to God and to others, is an important mark of a transformed life and an important pilgrim practice.

The Word Within

But how does this transformation occur? In verse 18, James says people are transformed into first fruits for God's service—that is, given birth into this new life—by the good gift of the word of truth. In fact, this may be the most important gift anyone can receive.

But what does James mean by the word of truth? How should this word transform us? And why is not doing what this word says like forgetting our own faces? While most of us could take a guess at the meaning of the term "the word of truth"—the Gospels, the Bible, the plan of salvation—taking a look deeper into the text reveals a surprising message.

James uses three phrases in this passage in reference to the same thing—"word of truth" in verse 18, "perfect law of freedom" in verse 25, and "the word planted in you" in verse 21. While the phrases "word of truth" and "perfect law" seem like typical biblical language to us, the phrase in verse 21, the "implanted word," seems out of the ordinary, but it is perhaps the most important phrase for deciphering James's message.

The term James uses for implanted word, the Greek word *emphutos*, is a scientific word not found often in Scripture. It literally means an object placed within another object by a scientific and natural process. It is an object that is inborn, that is within something else from its beginning.[3] This word is the word of truth and perfect law, the word that we are called not merely to hear to but to listen to and put into action. This word is not the text of one specific gospel, it is not in fact the Bible (although its message can be found in the Bible), and it is not a step-by-step plan of salvation.

This word is a message that was implanted within all of us at creation. While Jiminy Cricket calls it a conscience, many Christians call it the voice of the Holy Spirit. It is a message of truth, it is a message of perfection and freedom, and it has the ability to save us. In the context of James's letter to these churches, I think that he is not only speaking of the eternal salvation of human souls but of salvation from the kingdoms of this world, from a world of conflict, and from a world where the self comes first and leads to destruction. This implanted word within us is the knowledge that there is a God, that this God is Truth, and that God is moving in our world. It whispers to us that there is something beyond what we can see. It tells us we are not complete unless we have a relationship with God. This word leads us to live in the Way that Jesus taught us to live. And it has been with us the whole time; we might have simply forgotten about it.[4]

The genius in James's striking image—that forgetting this word is like forgetting what your own face looks like in a mirror—is that it tells us this implanted word is as much a part of us as our faces. To forget it, to fail to listen to it intently or act upon it, to refuse to let it save us or refuse to allow it to transform us into an offering for God is like forgetting a part of us (much worse than forgetting a birthday!). It is as absurd as forgetting something that is in front of us, within us, every day.

Without it we are not complete. From our physical births, we are given this gift of the message of salvation. We simply have to recognize it, to let it transform us, and it will give us a second birth into a new way of life—living as an offering to God! To do this, we recognize this word in the message of Jesus, in the words of the gospel, in the leadings of the Holy Spirit, and sometimes even in the lives of others.

How Easy to Forget

Like many things, however, we often find it easy to forget God's message of truth and freedom. Whether while serving as a youth minister, a hospital chaplain, or a pastor, I have always found it easy to become distracted and forget. When I served in the hospital, it was part of a temporary chaplaincy training program. I knew I would not serve in that capacity permanently, and as I worked there, I evaluated my next place of service. Would I go back to school? Did I feel called to be a senior pastor? These important life questions of ministry, along with financial worries, often distracted me from being a present and caring chaplain. I would find my-self simply going through the motions without putting my heart and soul into the ministry. I forgot God's message about freedom from the worries of the world and about salvation into a new way of life, and I turned my attention only to myself and my issues and away from the implanted word within me.

It is easy to forget.

But God told the Israelites in the Old Testament, "I will put my law on their minds, I will write it on their hearts" (Jer 31:33). God's message is within us all, ready to move the community of faith in directions we have never been before, ready to mold us as the first fruits for God, ready to make us into the types of communities and churches that God wants us to be.

This word calls us to action.

Perhaps it is calling us to seek ways to remove the bonds of racial segregation in our church bodies. Perhaps it is calling us to listen to one another, even those to whom it is hard to listen. Perhaps it is calling us to have more commitment in our prayer lives. Perhaps it is calling us to meet a need in our communities that others are neglecting. Perhaps it is calling us to open our hearts and minds to new ways of thinking about missions, discipleship, or worship. Perhaps it is calling us to live as a community of disciples, living missionally and offering this message of truth, freedom, and salvation to the world.

God calls churches to gather in anticipation of hearing a word from God. If we are open to the word of truth, the Spirit moves in and guides communities through worship, service, and communal discernment.[5] We are to listen to this word and let this word guide us, and if we do, God promises a blessing.

God's Missional Blessing

In our Christian world, the word "blessing" is often used carelessly. From the television sermons of "prosperity gospelers" to books such as *The Prayer of Jabez*, the idea of God's blessing is popular. We are told that if we are faithful enough and pure enough and prayerful enough, God will grant us health and wealth and success. But this message is not consistent with the gospel message, and certainly not with James. In fact, in verse 25, "Those who look intently at the perfect law of freedom, who listen to the word within us—who do it and do not forget it—they will be blessed *in what they do*," James indicates that it is not the person who will be blessed.

God does not promise to bless the person. In fact, as these persecuted churches and thousands of martyrs through the years could attest, doing God's word sometimes brings struggle and hardship.

God does not promise to bless us. Rather, God promises to bless our work and our mission. God's promised blessing is a missional blessing—a blessing to help disciples in our work of furthering God's mission in the world.

If we truly live as pilgrim people, a missional community dedicated to spreading the gospel, to helping those in need, and to participating in God's mission of saving the world—a church that looks outward at a broken world rather than inward at our own comforts and desires—God will bless what we do. That message should be more good news to us than any personal blessing we could hope for!

During recent visits to churches across the southeast, I heard many stories about ways these communities are becoming part of God's mission and witnessing the blessings of God in their mission opportunities. One church, after a period of listening, reflecting, and visioning, discerned that God was calling them to reach out to their community in ways that better embody a missional posture. The church renovated a house on its property, turning it into temporary lodging for families of international patients at a local hospital—their own version of a "Ronald McDonald House." The pastor recounted how one recent lodger from Africa, who had begun attending Sunday worship services, walked through the sanctuary on her last day in the United States, praying over the church and thanking God for the blessings she had received while her loved one was in the hospital. Because the church had reached out to her, she chose to spend her last day praying for this church and worshiping in its sanctuary. Everyone in the church, not only the visitors with hospitalized loved ones, was affected by this offer of hospitality. God blessed the congregation's ministry financially through a grant and spiritually as the church's mission was radically changed. This congregation did not forget the mission God had given them but committed to live lives transformed into offerings for God.

We are all called to be offerings—to be listeners and doers of the word, not only hearers, and not forgetters.

Sometimes we realize the very word we forgot was in us all along.

At creation, God planted a good gift, God's very word, within us. It is a word that offers truth and freedom, a word that leads to salvation. It is a word that calls us from within to action and that forms us into offerings to be used by God and blessed by God to change the world. However, the first thing we have to do is often the most difficult practice—simply to listen.

We have all we need to be disciples in the missional church. We have all we need for the pilgrim journey. In the end, we have no excuses.

The images in this passage of Scripture reveal an unusual and often overlooked pilgrim practice of Christian discipleship. Seeking to deepen our discipleship and sustain our pilgrimage as the missional community of God's church, we are to listen continuously to the word planted within us and allow it to transform our communities, our calling, and our mission. As we allow it to transform us into a people of action who live as disciples, we live no longer for ourselves but as an offering for God so that God's mission will be blessed through our journey.

6

Welcoming: Living Upside Down

My brothers and sisters, do you with your acts of favoritism really believe in our glorious Lord Jesus Christ? For if a person with gold rings and in fine clothes comes into your assembly, and if a poor person in dirty clothes also comes in, and if you take notice of the one wearing the fine clothes and say, "Have a seat here, please," while to the one who is poor you say, "Stand there," or, "Sit at my feet," have you not made distinctions among yourselves, and become judges with evil thoughts? Listen, my beloved brothers and sisters. Has not God chosen the poor in the world to be rich in faith and to be heirs of the kingdom that he has promised to those who love him? But you have dishonored the poor. Is it not the rich who oppress you? Is it not they who drag you into court? Is it not they who blaspheme the excellent name that was invoked over you? You do well if you really fulfill the royal law according to the scripture, "You shall love your neighbor as yourself." (James 2:1–8)

The congregation was made up of people from more than forty different nations—an international church in Europe with an explicit mission of openness, diversity, and hospitality. One such member was William, a thirty-nine-year-old mentally handicapped man who began attending the church's Sunday worship after his elderly mother, with whom he had lived, passed away. Sitting in the front pew, he brought a tape recorder every Sunday, continuously clicking the buttons on his recorder into play, fast-forward, rewind, and record. Often he mumbled incoherently and always he rocked back and forth as he clicked his recorder. After a few Sundays, a church member told William that he was making too much noise during the service and was becoming a distraction. This person told William that if he insisted on bringing his recorder and clicking the buttons, he should sit in the narthex where he could not disturb any other worshipers and listen to the service over the speakers. And so William did.

In a church made up of a diversity of bodies, ethnicities, nationalities, and ideologies, there was no room for one handicapped man who disturbed the others with his convulsive clatter. This story from Carol Bailey Stoneking is just one among thousands that could be told of people categorized in some way as "other," abandoned, forsaken, or even rejected by the church.[1]

Hospitality is, and always has been, a significant struggle in the church since its conception 2,000 years ago. In fact, struggles with hospitality were one of the first issues the early church had to deal with, according to Paul's letters, and they continue today: the debate over the inclusion of the Gentiles in the first century; the segregation of African Americans in the nineteenth and twentieth centuries; and arguments about the role of women or the welcoming of non-heterosexuals in the church in the twenty-first century. All these forms of exclusion are justified by an appeal to skewed interpretations of Scripture.

While the church has often failed to practice the radical welcome of Christ, it likewise often institutes an invisible practice of favoritism toward those who might provide some benefit for the congregation, continually discovering new reasons to favor certain groups of people over others, whether delineated by race, religion, sexual orientation, economic status, or social standing. Whether based on biological identities like male and female or social and financial differences, churches tend to accommodate the powerful and wealthy because of what they can do for us while neglecting those at the margins of society. Wealth gains a person import and influence, and while most churches may not be intentional in showing favoritism, such favoritism is an easy trap. Favoritism toward certain groups at the expense of exclusion of other groups is one of the primary hindrances to the radical welcome exhorted in James 2.

The Prince and the Pauper

As apparent in James's letter, which was written for a broad congregational audience in the first century, the issue of economic favoritism was a far-reaching problem that plagued many early church communities. In a short story of two verses, James reveals a great deal about the situation of the early church. It is the story of two men entering the assembly: one rich and the other poor. But the contextual details reveal even more. The church at this time is persecuted, a diaspora of communities facing oppression from the mighty Roman Empire. These churches are small, and in their attempts to survive, they seek protection and money. In other words, the early church is in need of wealthy benefactors. With money comes power and influence, and more power entails more protection. Activating a literal "When in Rome . . ." strategy through accommodation to the powers, or what theologian and civil rights advocate Howard Thurman describes as imitation, they absorb the culture and social behaviors of the dominant society. While they may gain imperial friendship, Thurman warns that such alliances may involve the repudiation of heritage, beliefs, and traditions—the stories and ethics that make a community distinct.[2]

It seems that the local church described in these verses is presented with an opportunity. A man arrives wearing a gold ring and fine clothes; more than a mere fashion statement, these adornments represented the regalia of a person of authority in Roman culture. A gold ring was often the symbol of a Roman nobleman or senator—a wealthy politician or government agent. This was not only a person of significant financial means but also one with a powerful political position in the empire. The term used for "fine clothes" in Greek is a word indicating a toga, which was often the garment worn by a political candidate. Suddenly the image begins to come together.[3]

It seems that a political candidate running for a position in the Roman Senate has approached the church, looking for a mutually beneficial partnership. Perhaps he promises the church additional protection and funding if the church will promise him the support of the "Christian voting base." It is a tempting alliance, and the church greets him with open arms, showing him special attention and offering him a prime seat.

Then a poor man enters the worship gathering wearing filthy clothes. He does not offer a mutually beneficial relationship. He does not offer political protection or an increased budget. All he offers is himself, someone who will probably require more from the church than anything he could possibly offer, and the congregation knows it.

He receives no special attention and is directed to a spot on the floor of the assembly. James's illustration goes beyond hospitality to warn about the dangers of church and state alliances. He says the church is a place where the amount of money one brings should not matter, the amount of influence one has has no relevance, and the entities of church and state should become not intertwined.

This story is the modern equivalent of a leading presidential candidate of the party of your choosing walking through the church doors one Sunday morning followed by a filthy and foul homeless person. While a friendly relationship with the candidate might offer the opportunity for more political sway or enriched resources, a relationship with the homeless man would offer none of this. Everywhere else in the world, these two men would receive completely different levels of hospitality, completely different welcomes. James says the church should be the one place where status, money, influence, and ability to help should have no relevance to how we view others—where all that matters is that both men were created in the image of God. But if we look at most of our churches today, I wonder, would this be the case? Do most churches repudiate the posture of hospitality throughout the story of Scripture (of Abraham and the three visitors, Jesus and Zacchaeus, Ruth and Naomi)[4] by the way we welcome (or fail to welcome) others?

Fake IDs

Favoritism is directly antithetical to the practice of hospitality. In the church, favoritism for any reason has no place. Believers, James says in 2:1, should not show favoritism. Then, following this vivid imagery, he offers reasons why favoritism has no part in the communal discipleship of the church.[5]

James identifies his readers as those who "believe in our glorious Christ Jesus" (2:1). Examination of the Greek text, however, reveals a slight textual difference. The Greek text literally reads "those who hold the faith of your Lord Jesus Christ." While this may not seem like an important distinction, the phrase "faith of Christ" is imperative to understanding this passage and its message for the church.[6] Christians not only place faith *in* Christ, but over and over again, the Bible states that God saves us through the faith *of* Christ. Our faith participates in the faith of Christ. We are justified not by our own works, not even exclusively by our own faith, but by "the faith of Jesus Christ." Better translations of this phrase suggest that the preposition in this genitive construction is more accurately rendered possessive. The faith of Jesus—the faith it took to go all the way to the cross—is the salvifically significant event, not anything we can do on our own, not even anything we believe on our own! This does not mean that trust in Christ is not important, but it shifts the focus to the works and faithfulness of Christ.[7]

As the Christ who had enough faith in his mission to become human via an unwed teenager, to invite lowly fishermen to join him as partners in ministry, to go all the way to the cross, Jesus allows us to participate in that faith. In times when our faith wanes or we find it difficult to believe in much of anything, the faith of Christ is always present. Like the word placed within each of us, the faith of Christ becomes my own faith as I share in his unconditional grace and loyalty. Christians share in the bold and strong faith of Jesus, and this is a faith that had no place for favoritism. It saw everyone as equal and as someone created in the image of God. If the faith of Jesus had no room for favoritism, then as participants in that faith, we have no room for it either. We witness to the faith of Christ through the way we welcome everyone indiscriminately, that is, through the practice of hospitality. This faith dictates a pilgrim practice of radical welcome.

James then takes it a step further. We not only participate in the faith of Christ but our very identity is in Christ. In his claim that the rich slander the "excellent name that was invoked over you," he makes a statement about the identity of the church and its people. The "name invoked over you" is a reference to the name of Christ spoken over believers during their baptism.[8] James is saying that through conversion and baptism, through participation in the church, Christians are not only given the faith of Christ but also given a new name and a new identity. We participate in the faith of Christ, and we belong to Christ. Our new identity is in him. Baptism is more than a symbol of some invisible, inner transformation; it is an initiation into a whole new identity, a new community, a new existence, even a new creation.[9] Bonhoeffer suggested that baptism actually effects a radical break with the ways of the world. "In baptism," he wrote, "I am deprived of my immediate relationship to the given realities

of the world, since Christ the mediator and Lord has ste
me and the world. Those who are baptized no longer be'
The event of baptism means to "see our life and all thing.
new and free way."[10] In this way, it is a dangerous political act tha.
our associations and allegiances (I will explore this further in chapter y,
"Witnessing").

For many, our identity as American, as successful, as white, black, or
Hispanic, as rich or poor defines us—perhaps even supersedes our faith
identity. Perhaps our religion matters for our spiritual lives, but not for
how we see ourselves and others socially, economically, or politically. I
have come to believe that we spend most of our lives seeking or forming identity. We are labeled from the time we are young, and it does not
take long for us to assign labels ourselves. Then we spend our lives either
succumbing to these descriptions of being "other" or trying desperately
to break free from them. By identifying ourselves according to race or
nationality, it also becomes easier to hate, oppress, or even kill others—
as in American slavery, Rwandan genocide, or the contemporary fear of
Islam—destroying a sense of common humanity under God.

These imposed identities haunt us and determine our behavior toward others until we finally realize that none of them matter—that all
previous identities fall away when we become a Christian and our identity
is in the one who sacrificed himself for us, the one who loved us unconditionally. Our identity is in Christ. As theologian John Howard Yoder
articulated, in baptism "all prior given or chosen identities are transcended."[11] We are no longer able to use people's distinctiveness to separate,
discriminate, or exclude them. These prior identities and their ruthless
holds on us fade away in comparison to the new name of Christian!

When we enter into the church community, into a relationship
with God, we no longer belong to the world; we belong to Christ, and
our identity is in him. (Paul echoes this message beautifully in Galatians
3:26–28—"For in Christ you are all children of God through faith . . . .
There is no longer Jew or Greek, there is no longer slave or free, there is
no longer male and female; for you are all one in Christ.") When we are
no longer identified by race, gender, nationality, or immigration status,
these imposed identities become nothing but meaningless afterthoughts.
Therefore, there is no reason to tell someone she is not capable of performing a job as minister because of her gender, to feel animosity toward

the family down the street because of where they came from or how they arrived here, or to feel morally superior to my coworker because he is in love with someone of the same sex. Likewise, there is no reason to show favoritism to those who look like me, seem to fit in better, or have the power or resources to help. Radical hospitality becomes available for all.

Reality Upside Down

This new identity changes everything (someone once wrote that it, in fact, makes everything new)! It incorporates us into a new reality, as part of a new kingdom. In verse 5, James makes a difficult statement that it is the poor who will inherit the kingdom of God. This shocking proclamation moves counter to the existing trajectory of our consumerist culture; the poor usually inherit nothing. It is a complete reversal of all of our known economic and social structures. It is an upheaval of the capitalist impulses that drive our desires and work ethic. James's proclamation might even make some of us angry. The poor are blessed and the rich are warned. It doesn't make sense.

In words that echo the Sermon on the Mount, where in the Gospel of Luke Jesus says, "Blessed are the poor for they shall inherit the kingdom of God," James describes a kingdom that does not mesh with our sensibilities of fairness.[12] This is a kingdom founded upon an ethic of openness and a practice of hospitality, based on God's welcome and embrace of all creation. Writer Donald Kraybill calls it an "Upside Down Kingdom"—a reversal of the ways of the world.[13] As the crowd said of the Christians in Thessalonica, they "have turned the world upside down" (Acts 17:6, KJV). Discipleship for a missional church is a calling to live upside down, to witness to the upside-down kingdom of God, to embody its new economic and social postures in our church communities. We are no longer under the rule of self-interest.

The primary law in this new reality, this new kingdom, is the commandment to love your neighbor as yourself. In verse 8, James quotes the "royal law," as our Bibles translate it—or literally the "law of our King," the law of the kingdom of God.[14] Within our church communities, living in the "Upside Down Kingdom," and as disciples of Jesus, we are to put others first with the same sacrificial love of Christ who died for the very ones who had him killed—who died for us, we who betray him every single day. That is the attitude, the overarching rule in the Upside Down Kingdom.

It is the way of life—a way of living counter-culturally to the way of the world. Others come first, the poor are rewarded, the rich are warned. It is a way of life where favoritism has no place. This new kingdom, this new identity, should affect the way we live, the way we view other people, and the way we treat others.

It is important to note again that James was writing in and for the context of Christian community. His exhortations to a radical form of welcome are more easily accomplished when an entire community decides to undertake this mission. In other words, it is easy to forget or become distracted, and remembering requires a community that continuously reminds one another that their identity is in Christ. It takes a church on mission together to live upside down, to become the Body of Christ. In his examination of the first disciples in the Gospel of Matthew, James McClendon suggested that while discipleship certainly entails obedience, it also means solidarity with one another.[15] Disciples cannot exist alone, and disciples cannot exist at the exclusion of others.

The practice of hospitality, inviting others into the worshiping community, to the Communion table, into the *ubuntu* of fellowship, is an invitation to become one Body. That is what it means to be the Body of Christ, where the body is incomplete if one part is missing. Author and atheist-turned-minister Sara Miles captures this truth beautifully as she reflects on her initiation into the church: "[Baptism] had eroded my identity as a journalist and given me an unsettling glimpse of how very little I knew. I was no less flawed or frightened or capable of being hurt than I'd been before . . . and now, in addition, I was adrift in this water, yoked together with all kinds of other Christians, many of whom I didn't like or trust."[16]

Baptism into that "noble name" incorporates individual members into one Body, not where differences go away, but where diversity becomes a reason for inclusion, fellowship, and worship. It is a Body where the power of these differences is no longer an identity maker but only something that strengthens the community as one. As the Body of Christ, the church exists and witnesses to God's presence on earth. It witnesses to the radical, unconditional welcome God extends to all God's people. Mary McClintock Fulkerson suggested that such practices make it possible for "once invisible" people, like the poor man in James's parable, to appear.[17] Just like the other pilgrim practices, the practice of radical hospitality is simply an extension and imitation of God's character. It images the Trinitarian quality of a God who is three relationships in one—a God who is a community of equal relationships. If the church expects to witness to this pure hospitality, it cannot practice the exclusion or favoritism of anyone.

Becoming One Body

Breaking down the false identities that divide. Overturning the stereotypes, prejudices, and favoritism that keep us from showing the world a new Way. Realizing that there can be no more discrimination because Christ died for all.[18] Seeing others as people created in the image of God and worthy of love and peace. Bringing others into fellowship with a triune God who welcomes all. Transforming churches into communities on pilgrimage that share a new reality and a new name with the world. Becoming a people who follow the person who showed us what it means to love unconditionally.

In a world where people are welcomed or rejected based on a myriad of factors—race, economic level, social status—the church stands out because we practice a radical welcome and inclusiveness that sees others not as means to an end, but as people created in the image of our Lord. These are essential practices of discipleship.

"The church, as those called out by God," noted Hauerwas and Willimon, "embodies a social alternative that the world cannot on its own terms know."[19] This is not a natural, democratic, or commonsense social ethic. As a contrast society, it is up to us to show the world a new way, to help it realize that a new reality is possible where favoritism, social hierarchy, and oppression can cease to exist. In this vein, the practice of radical welcome has an intrinsic evangelistic impulse. Through life together as the missional community of God, we are Christ's hands and feet; that is, we are God's witnesses to the world of the royal law of love, inviting everyone to join us in God's grand mission. Christians demonstrate hospitality (along with other pilgrim practices) by being the church, "that is, by being something the world is not," continued Hauerwas and Willimon, "a place, clearly visible to the world, in which people are faithful to their promises, love their enemies, tell the truth, honor the poor, suffer for righteousness, and thereby testify to the amazing community-creating power of God."[20] The church should be a place defined not by favoritism and accommodation but by inclusive and equal hospitality.

Pilgrim practices, therefore, are not the same as the practices of those seeking to change public policy, of those for whom favoritism is a way of life. Hospitality is not meant for the few or the powerful. The church does not need to, and should never, accommodate to those in power positions, as exemplified in the ecclesial tale in James 2. It does not seek power through financial or political alliances. Jesus established his kingdom on the margins of society as a witness to the world. Ours is not a pilgrimage to achieve political influence, as James warns.[21] The kingdom of God is not achieved on Capitol Hill or in the voting booth. Nor will it break through from the ringing bell of Wall Street. It will break through, instead, in the smallest, most subversive acts.

During the second week in which William was forced to sit in the narthex during the service, Stoneking's story continues, Miss Ida was unusually late for worship. Miss Ida was a matriarch of the church, a sophisticated, prim elderly lady. When she saw William sitting in the narthex alone, she inquired about his odd choice of location. When he told her what the church member had said about his distracting behavior, Miss Ida decided to join him in the narthex for the service. The next Sunday during worship, ten worshipers joined him in the narthex, and the next Sunday, thirty sat with him. Today, because of the subversive, radical welcome of one woman, an entire congregation sees hospitality much differently than before. William now sits in the choir with his recorder, clicking the buttons continuously, rocking back and forth to the rhythms of the hymns and sermon. Then, every Sunday after church, he walks the few miles to his mother's grave and leaves the recording of that morning's service with the words, "Here's church, Mama."

William brings his mother "church"—not the simple recordings of a Sunday liturgy but the event of embodiment, of becoming a Body composed of many different bodies—some broken, some old—but all making one Body of Christ where all are welcome. In sum, church is the practice of physically extending God's radical welcome to the world. As Miles reflected on her experience of welcome, "We were dying to our individual selves and becoming a body. It had sore places and unhealed scars; it wasn't perfect, but it was beautiful. It was Christ's body, or as we said in church, a church."[22]

7

Committing: Gone off the Deep End

WHAT GOOD IS IT, *my brothers and sisters, if you say you have faith but do not have works? Can faith save you? If a brother or sister is naked and lacks daily food, and one of you says to them, "Go in peace; keep warm and eat your fill," and yet you do not supply their bodily needs, what is the good of that? So faith by itself, if it has no works, is dead.*

But someone will say, "You have faith and I have works." Show me your faith without works, and I by my works will show you my faith. You believe that God is one; you do well. Even the demons believe—and shudder. Do you want to be shown, you senseless person, that faith without works is barren?

Was not our ancestor Abraham justified by works when he offered his son Isaac on the altar? You see that faith was active along with his works, and faith was brought to completion by the works. Thus the scripture was fulfilled that says, "Abraham believed God, and it was reckoned to him as righteousness," and he was called the friend of God. You see that a person is justified by works and not by faith alone. Likewise, was not Rahab the prostitute also justified by works when she welcomed the messengers and sent them out by another road? For just as the body without the spirit is dead, so faith without works is also dead. (James 2:14–26)

It was a steamy North Carolina summer night. Hundreds of people from churches all over town crowded into the stiff pews of our small sanctuary to hear the renowned out-of-town traveling evangelist who had come to preach for five nights in our annual revival. I cannot remember which night it was—I was only seven—but I do remember I was bored. The loud projections of the preacher were nothing but background noise as I sat in the pew beside my mother and colored pictures on the paper bulletin. I was simply a child, caught in my own world of dinosaurs and spaceships, when I heard the preacher say the one word that always grasped my attention—*Hell*. Every time he said it, he got louder. Every time he said it, it seemed he was speaking directly to me.

I looked up. Hell was a place of eternal torment. Fire and suffering. You would be separated from God, which is bad enough. But even worse for a seven-year-old boy, you might be separated from those you love—even from your parents. But for those poor lost souls who want to escape the eternal damnation of hell, that night could be the night! It was as if I could feel the devil's pitchfork poking me in the heels, urging me toward the front. There was no need to have a forty-five-minute altar call that evening; as soon as the preacher bowed his head to pray, I was heading down the aisle, leaving hell in the dust, going toward I-didn't-know-what. All I had to do was believe, the preacher said, and in that moment I'd have believed anything he told me to.

This rather snarky tale of my "conversion" is not to say that all revivals, traveling evangelists, or fire-and-brimstone sermons ought to be described with as much cynicism. It is not to say that all emotional religious experiences are bad or all similar evangelistic efforts create such shallow believers as I was as an adolescent. I am saying, however, that cheap faith and shallow discipleship are a deep and infectious problem in today's North American churches—and not just for prepubescent enthusiasts wanting to stay out of the eternal flames! Our churches are filled with members—adolescents and adults—who assent to the right set of orthodox beliefs but have never truly been transformed. They are victims, or perhaps perpetrators, of what Bonhoeffer called "cheap grace."[1] They are not yet on the pilgrim journey of discipleship. They have not yet developed the habits and practices of faith. But is correct belief not enough? Are we not saved by faith?

These questions lead to the heart of any endeavor to examine what discipleship truly means. They also lead to the most controversial part of our guidebook, James 2:14–25—the section often inappropriately labeled "Faith versus Works." James concludes this section in verse 24 with the statement, "faith without works is dead." It is the section that made Reformer Martin Luther want to leave this "epistle of straw" out of the canon. It is a section that causes many to place James in opposition to Paul: is it grace through faith, or our works that save us? Following James's structure thus far, we see he began with faith in James 1, then moved to the power of the implanted word and asked his readers to be "doers of that word." He began James 2 with a discussion of congregational ethics and now approaches the connection between faith and works—in other words, what it means to be a doer of the word.

Does James contradict Paul? Are their views of faith and discipleship opposed? What does that mean for pilgrims trying to follow the narrow, risky path of discipleship? In this chapter, I will examine the images James uses to explain the relationship between faith and works and will locate their convergence in the practice of commitment.

Faith versus Works

Now, 2,000 years after James wrote this sermon letter, and 500 years after Luther's scorn, Christians still argue over faith versus works, or orthodoxy (right belief) versus orthopraxy (right practice). It reminds me of the old riddle, "Which came first, the chicken or the egg?" Which is more essential for discipleship, faith or works? Emerging church leaders like Brian McLaren emphasize orthopraxy as an often missing part of our understanding of the church and Christian life—and justifiably so. As I indicated at the beginning of this chapter, from my experience as a congregational minister, shallow faith is as much an epidemic in our churches as people who think all you need to do is be a "good person." We intellectually assent to all the right things, but it does not change our behavior; we do not *practice* the faith. In the introduction to his somewhat controversial book *A Generous Orthodoxy*, McLaren admittedly outlines, "This book sees orthopraxy as the point of orthodoxy . . . a point so unorthodox as to encourage a good many readers to abandon this book right now."[2] There has been much attention given (and there have been many books written) recently in theology and congregational life about the practice of Christian life as an essential part of our Christian formation. In fact, James himself seems to indicate that orthopraxy is more important than orthodoxy in this chapter. In verse 19 he says that even demons believe the basic truths about God. Even the demons are orthodox, he says! So what good does that do us?

It seems clear what side of the argument James falls on. A person is justified by works and not faith alone (2:24)? Demons are orthodox? No wonder Martin Luther wanted to toss this letter from the canon.

Closely examining what James is describing here, however, leads me to wonder if his detractors oversimplify his message. Perhaps faith and works are not like the chicken and the egg. Perhaps demons are not actually orthodox, if we begin to understand what *orthodox* means. Maybe James is arguing against a false dichotomy here. Faith and works are not two disparate concepts; they cannot be separated. Orthodoxy necessitates orthopraxy, and orthopraxy contains orthodoxy. True faith contains works, and works are no good without faith! Rather than arguing for the primacy of one over the other, James is saying that the two are utterly indistinguishable. Barth is helpful here in his extended discussion of faith in *Church Dogmatics*. While certainly eschewing any form of "works righteousness," Barth integrated Paul and James by describing faith as *obedience*. "Faith differs from any mere thinking and believing and knowing, or indeed from any other trusting," he suggested, "in the fact that it is an obeying."[3] Faith, in fact, is an imitation of Christ in his humility and obedience to the Father. It is a response to the reality and existence of human beings as a people who are justified by God, and in this way, it is how we participate in God.[4]

In light of Barth's harmonization, it seems that Paul and James were not arguing two different positions. Rather, they had two distinct purposes and audiences. Paul, as a missionary to the unevangelized, emphasizes faith as central to becoming a disciple—much as James does in James 1. And James, as he writes to churches full of Christians who have fallen into moral relativism, argues for the importance of works in their understanding of community and discipleship. The two perspectives are seeking the same ultimate goal in the end. In fact, in Ephesians 2:10, right after he writes that we are saved by grace through faith, Paul asserts that we were "created in Christ Jesus for *good works*, which God prepared beforehand to be our way of life"—our Way of discipleship.

Is Faith Not Enough?

Paul and James both proclaim that faith cannot exist apart from works.[5] James goes so far as to say that faith works together with works and in fact is completed "out of" works (2:22). Faith is "co-working with works."[6] Actions do not substitute for right beliefs or attitude. Instead, "the actions reveal the attitude and make it alive," says James scholar Luke Timothy Johnson.[7] Faith without works is dead—it is barren and empty—because it is not true faith, James contends (2:20). This false faith is empty because it does not rely upon the implanted word (1:27), the word that lies within, that gives life, that fills, that offers salvation into a new story of new existence and new community, that guides the community of faith as we seek to follow the Way of Jesus.

In C. S. Lewis's children's novel *The Silver Chair* in *The Chronicles of Narnia* series, some of the characters begin to doubt the existence of the great lion Aslan and the land called Narnia. As they discuss their dwindling faith in the midst of the gloomy Kingdom of Underland, the defiant character Puddleglum tells Underland's Witch Queen, "Suppose we have only dreamed, or made up, all those things . . . . Suppose we have. Suppose this black pit of a kingdom of yours is the only world . . . . Then all I can say is the made-up things seem a good deal more important than the real ones!" After more discussion he concludes, "I'm on Aslan's side even if there isn't any Aslan to lead it. I'm going to live as like a Narnian as I can even if there isn't any Narnia!"[8] Even if the evidence points otherwise, Puddleglum's practices of faith—his works—will carry him through. Faith and works work together. Even when one begins to fade, even so slightly, the other can pick us back up and set us on the Way. In the end, they are two perspectives within the same reality, the same calling, the same journey.

Again, James offers vivid imagery to guide us on the Way. He turns to the Hebrew Scriptures, recalling the works—and the faith—of Abraham and Rahab. Neither could have done the things they did—Abraham taking his son Isaac to be sacrificed on Mt. Moriah and Rahab helping the Hebrew spies in Jericho—without faith. Their faith was exhibited through their mighty works, and that faith was credited as righteousness. (Because of his faith James also calls Abraham a "friend of God," a term unique to James. I will examine this phrase in more detail in chapter 9, "Witnessing.") With these images James connects his message to the larger story of the Jews and the mission of God. Faith and works have always worked together to connect God's people with God. True orthodoxy entails orthopraxy and vice versa. They both are essential and inseparable for a life of discipleship.

These illustrations of a man and woman demonstrating exemplary faith and works are juxtaposed with another image of a man and woman in verse 15. Similar to the poor man in 2:2, this brother and sister have nothing—no clothes or food. This symbolizes the utter depths of destitution in the biblical world. These two are the poorest of the poor. For James, it seems true faith is demonstrated specifically by the formation of communities that show hospitality to the poor, communities that demonstrate the presence of Christ, communities we call the church. These two indigent persons come to the church community seeking refuge, clothing, and food. Scholars tell us that every Jewish synagogue—and presumably every Jewish-Christian church—maintained a "pauper's dish" to meet the emergency needs of beggars.[9] The church in this story presumably has the means to aid. Instead of leading the beggars to the pauper's dish, or offering food or money, the church leaders simply offer a blessing, "Go in peace," which is terrific religious language but nothing that actually helps the situation of the impoverished folk. In reading this story, I am reminded of a quote attributed to church father St. Basil: "When someone strips a man of his clothing, we call him a thief. And one who might clothe the naked and does not, should he not be given the same name?" Indifference to suffering is just as bad as causing it ourselves.

What is more interesting is that this blessing of peace—used in the beginning of several New Testament letter greetings, was also the liturgy spoken at the end of Holy Communion in the early church.[10] After the church community had finished their meal of thanksgiving, celebrating the body and bread of Christ broken and given away for the sake of all humanity, the community neglected to give away their own selves for the sake of the poor. The action that was supposed to unite the church as the one Body of Christ and then send it out for service, the meal that literally *embodies* hospitality—the Eucharist, or Communion—was used as a means of exclusion and inhospitality. James has a way with irony! Our identity as the church—the Body of Christ—compels us to act like the Body of Christ, to give of ourselves continually for the sake of others (see Phil 2:5–11). This is what James means by works that make faith complete. The faith of this community in James's story is a faith without works, a faith that does not seek the word within, a faith that is shallow and treads lightly on any notion of true discipleship.

The Deep End

A church that does not demonstrate works of faith has no faith at all. In the first century, James was attempting to remedy a problem that still pervades our churches—shallow faith. Too often it seems, Christians in America, especially those of us who call ourselves evangelical, become so caught up in reaching the "lost" and sharing the news of Christ initially that we neglect the deeper and more difficult Great Commission to develop disciples. Many churches emphasize the conversion experience to the neglect of the truly amazing thing about grace—transformation—while other churches focus exclusively on works neglecting the point that it is faith in Christ as Lord that constitutes works as *Christian* practices in the first place. Following Christ is more than a decision and more than doing good things. It is accepting our true identity that has been within us from the beginning (remember the "implanted word"?) and allowing this identity change to transform people and communities. It is committing to a pilgrim journey, a practice that, like believing, may require daily renewal!

To some degree, this neglect of discipleship is the result of shoddy evangelism—scare tactics (like those at my revival conversion), massive and emotional altar calls, or programmatic conversations intended to lead to a "key question" about eternal destinations—or, just as harmful, no evangelism at all. While committed Christians have certainly emerged from these types of experiences, most of these evangelical conversion efforts are aimed primarily at generating large numbers of converts and often do not cultivate the depth of commitment that James is seeking in his letter.

I remember speaking at a youth camp one spring. This camp often encouraged speakers to offer extended, emotional invitations, especially on the final night—"Altar-Call Night." It was one of my first youth evangelism sermons, and I told myself that I was not going to offer an invitation to a shallow faith. The time came for the altar call at the end of the sermon, and I was supposed to explain how the youth might respond and invite them to come forward if they wanted to make any decisions. As I began to pray, I could hear the guitarist behind me playing soft, slow notes, inspiring memories of similar emotion-filled invitations in my own youth. I could feel myself being drawn back into that safe time and that comfortable framework of faith. I felt the music urge me toward an emotional appeal, and I began to envision multitudes of youth storming the front of the sanctuary. Then I looked out at the children and teenagers. I knew I could not offer them an invitation to cheap grace. In fact, I did not want to make the decision an easy one. I did not want that walk down the center aisle to be a leisurely stroll leading to an inconsequential decision. I wanted it to be a difficult walk, a walk of commitment, a walk of cross carrying, the first anxious step in a long and treacherous pilgrimage. I wanted the youth to know what their decision that night might truly mean—that it was not just a one-time decision but a lifelong commitment to be a part of a particular (and peculiar) people and movement.

Faith is a commitment to a certain way of life and a certain type of community that changes everything.

Needless to say, after spending a few minutes explaining how difficult this commitment was, a costly commitment of self-sacrifice and self-denial, I had only a handful of youth walk down to the front. I am still waiting for an invitation to come back and speak at that camp again!

The message of costly grace is a message we don't like to hear. It is a message I'm sure James's readers did not like either. However, it is a truth essential to our life together.

Faith is not meant to be easy. Faith is life giving but also life taking. It is ultimate fulfillment but ultimate self-emptying at the same time. It is joyous and treacherous. It is certainly about right beliefs, but it is just as much about right practices because the two cannot be separated. Faith and works are unified in our new life as the church community. True faith is a practice of commitment, a continued daily (and on some days, hourly) dedication to be part of God's mission and work in the world through the church. As I illustrated earlier in chapter 4, "Believing," true belief begins with a new vision of reality, a new way of seeing the world. The practice of commitment often starts with a difficult walk down the aisle, and it should continue as a difficult walk of life that is a pilgrimage with crosses on our backs. More than a decision or a doctrine, it is a brand-new identity as part of the Body of Christ and a new way of life that we call discipleship.

Donald Miller summed up the point well in his book *Blue Like Jazz.* "What I believe is not what I say I believe; what I believe is what I do," he wrote. "Living for something is the hard thing. Living for something extends beyond fashion, glory, or recognition. We live for what we believe."[11]

8

Speaking Wisely:
The Myth of Sticks and Stones

If we put bits into the mouths of horses to make them obey us, we guide their whole bodies. Or look at ships: though they are so large that it takes strong winds to drive them, yet they are guided by a very small rudder wherever the will of the pilot directs. So also the tongue is a small member, yet it boasts of great exploits.

How great a forest is set ablaze by a small fire! And the tongue is a fire. The tongue is placed among our members as a world of iniquity; it stains the whole body, sets on fire the cycle of nature, and is itself set on fire by hell. For every species of beast and bird, of reptile and sea creature, can be tamed and has been tamed by the human species, but no one can tame the tongue—a restless evil, full of deadly poison. With it we bless the Lord and Father, and with it we curse those who are made in the likeness of God. From the same mouth come blessing and cursing. My brothers and sisters, this ought not to be so. (James 3:3–10)

I distinctly remember one day in seminary sitting in an introductory class of around 200 students in a large auditorium. As I took my seat toward the back next to my friend—who will remain nameless for his protection—we both realized that a teaching assistant was lecturing in the professor's absence. We exchanged looks and discussed, rather loudly, our impending boredom (ironic, as I currently inhabit a similar position as a teaching assistant!). Resigned to "wasting" the next hour, we sat down, opened our newspapers, and began reading as the fledgling lecturer spoke. During the class, we evaded our boredom by vociferously ridiculing the assistant's uncomfortable attempts at jokes, his accent (a true case of the pot calling the kettle black), and his awkward demeanor. We were brutal!

At the midway point, my eyes lifted from my newspaper when I heard him say, "I would like to thank my wife for coming today. She is sitting right over there." He pointed to the seat directly adjacent to mine, where she had been sitting the whole time within eyeshot and earshot of our antics. After swiftly pulling our feet out of our mouths, we immediately dropped the papers to the floor, sat up straight, and listened with astonishing attentiveness. After the lecture ended—which in retrospect was highly insightful—we sang praises about the assistant's pointed articulation, incisive wisdom, and refreshing wit purposefully loud enough for his wife to hear. I never discovered if he learned of our behavior, but I was ashamed that day not that I had gotten "caught" but that my friend and I had not used our words wisely. We had spoken harsh words, making fun of someone who was only trying to help immature divinity students—and future pastors—learn a thing or two about theology.

The popular saying that parents all over the world tell their children, "Sticks and stones may break my bones, but words can never hurt me," may be one of the biggest lies of our time. Words can and do hurt: "whites only," "this marriage is over," "I don't love you," "why do you always disappoint me?" We have all felt the effects of hurtful words. Just like physical scars, they leave a deep and lasting imprint. Sometimes we never recover. Hurtful words rip apart lives, friendships, families, and churches.

Being a leader in the fledgling church, James had witnessed the devastating effects of harsh words. He saw churches in disorder, in chaos, in rage. James knew that true wisdom is exemplified in the way people speak and behave, and he knew that the tongue is the key to good and right living. Engaging a theme also at the heart of Jesus' teachings, James wrote to his congregations about the power of such a small instrument as the tongue.

Size Doesn't Matter

James again makes his point using two vivid images. His letter is like a sermon and could be preached by a messenger to these congregations in about fifteen minutes. (Shouldn't most of us preachers follow James' example?) Here in typical sermonic style, he offers his readers illustrations with which they could connect. The first is of a horse and a bit. A bit is a tiny instrument placed in the mouth of a horse and attached to the reigns in order for the rider to control the horse's movements. As a bit is a small piece of equipment but controls the entire direction of a large animal, James says the tongue is also a small body part but with great power. In fact, it can completely control a person, take over, and make people say words they can never take back.

James then compares the tongue to the rudder of a ship. In the same way, a rudder is a small part of the ship but has great controlling power; it can turn and direct the movement of the entire ship. While this example may appear to be the same as the previous one, it has an added dimension. In Christian literature, the ship has often been a symbol of the church, and this symbol was likely used during the time of James. In this metaphor, James is speaking of the danger and power of speech not only on an individual level but also on a corporate, congregational level.[1] As the church (local and universal), our speech also carries great weight. How we speak and present ourselves to the world—how we proclaim and witness to the gospel—determines the way the world views us. Numerous studies indicate the most-cited reason people view Christians negatively is hypocrisy—how we use our words and fail to back them up. Navigating through a world that is stormy and windy, with many temptations and struggles, the way Christians speak to each other and to those outside our faith is of utmost importance. Even a small group of people, or a few insignificant words, can have a great impact on the direction we travel in our journey.

Years ago, I spent an entire summer learning vocabulary words. I was studying for the GRE and knew that in order to get into a specific academic program, I had to make a certain score on the verbal section of the test. I bought two study books, each packed with vocabulary words. I had taken the test once and fallen short of my verbal goal, so I decided to buckle down and study hard. Over the period of a month I memorized 3,500 words—from "acanthocephalan" to "zygomorphic." My self-satisfaction was fleeting, however, as my newfound knowledge quickly dissipated. (If you asked me what three-fourths of those words mean now, except for the ones I looked up again to use in this illustration, I could not even begin to tell you!)

According to the Oxford English Dictionary, there are more than 600,000 words in the English language. In reality, no one should struggle to find the right words to say to someone. So why is it that often we do not choose the right words? Why is it that often we choose the harsh word or the angry word? Why is it that so often we choose the word that we immediately wish we could take back?

Not only do the actual words we use have great power but also the ways we use them. Experts say that 90 percent of information is communicated nonverbally, through body language. This means the manner in which we say things—our tone, posture, hand movements, and facial expressions—is just as important as the content of what we say.

I heard a story of a Methodist bishop who got a call one day from an elder of one of his congregations who was having problems with her pastor. "He's arrogant and prideful," she told him. "He thinks he knows more than the rest of us. He tells us we are going to hell!" The bishop investigated the situation and found out, among other things, that what the preacher had been telling them—that they were going to hell—didn't in all respects seem far from the truth! Regardless, in order to alleviate the situation, he decided to move the pastor to another church and brought in a new pastor for this congregation. A few months later he called the same elder to ask how things were going. "Oh, we love him," the elder said. "He tells us we are going to hell." Confused, the bishop asked her, "If he tells you the same thing, why do you like him so much?" After a moment of silence, she responded, "Because when he tells us, he has tears in his eyes."

Both of James's images, the horse and the ship, require a driver—a jockey or captain. While James compared the bit and the rudder to the tongue, he failed to identify the captain in the metaphor. This intentional omission reminds the reader that the choice of driver is up to us. In other words, to whom are we going to give control of our tongues?

Toward the end of James 3, he relates speech to the idea of wisdom. He writes of wisdom from above—the wisdom of God. The wisdom of God is manifest through wise speech, while hurtful speech comes from evil itself. We are involved in a deep struggle, and Christians have the choice to give control of our tongues to God or to evil.

Who will be our captain? The choice is up to us.

The Worth of an Image

James summarizes his point, "With the same mouth we both praise God and curse men. This should not be!" (3:10). It should not be easy to praise God and then curse someone created in the image of God. However, Christians do this every single day, and sometimes without realizing the grave contradiction. It's easy to call out the person who cuts me off in traffic, the telemarketer who phones during dinner, the umpire who calls me out at first base. While the primary message of this section is to warn of the dangers of an unbridled tongue, it is also an important message about the value of the person.

In Genesis 1:26, God creates humans, all humans, in the image of God. Readers, however, often gloss over this in Scripture and interpret the image of God as indicating humans have a soul, free will, or the capacity to reason. I think Scripture means something much deeper when it says we were all created in the image of God. It not only means we all have a restlessness inside of us to be with God but also means that now, in whatever form or situation, we have value—an importance that only God grants. "You formed my innermost parts, you wove me in my mother's womb," the psalmist says in Psalm 139. God created every single person on the earth and calls every person to join God's mission. God created us to be images of God on the earth. Whether we find ourselves falling away time after time, whether we think we could not get any lower or could not possibly do anything worse than what we have just done, whether we see ourselves as a lost cause or beyond hope, God proclaims that we are all special—all images of God!

This truth should affect both the way we view ourselves and also the way we see others. There is a lot of talk in public debate about the sanctity of or right to life. Life, however, is not a right or value in and of itself. This legal framework shortcuts the depth of God's immense love for creation. Life is not a "right"; it is a gift, and our lives, our bodies, and our personalities are valuable because God created them.

When we talk about a coworker behind his back, we tarnish the image of God.

When we condescendingly avoid the homeless person on the street as beneath us or worthless, we diminish the image of God.

When we speak out in anger to a family member, we attack the image of God.

When we terminate the potential of someone else's gift of life—both the unborn baby *and* the criminal on death row—we destroy the image of God.

There is a struggle going on for control of our tongues, our hearts, and our lives. When we struggle and fight against each other, when we argue and speak harshly, we are attacking ourselves and resisting God. We are fighting against the one who wants to lead us to wisdom, the one who created us all in God's image. It makes no sense, James asserts. "This ought not to be so!"

The Worth of Words

I once heard popular speaker Tony Campolo tell a story about the time he was a counselor at a middle-school boys' camp.[2] A boy in his cabin, Billy, was physically handicapped. He dragged his body while he walked in awkward movements, and his speech perpetually slurred. Of course, all the other teenage boys picked on him the entire week. When Billy talked to them, they mocked him, replying in slurred speech and awkward hand motions. On Thursday morning, Billy's cabin was selected to lead camp devotions, and his cabin mates voted him to be the speaker. They thought it would be funny to watch him struggle to speak in front of the camp. Before Campolo could stop the spectacle, he realized that Billy was thrilled about the opportunity. He dragged himself up on the stage, and in between spasms and stutterings, with laughs coming from the audience, Billy took almost a half minute to say, "Je-sus . . . loves . . . me . . . and I . . . l-love . . . Jesus." When he finished, there was silence. As Campolo looked over the crowd, he saw middle school boys with tears on their cheeks. A revival broke out in camp that week, Campolo explained, because of one handicapped boy who was "not normal," who was willing to get up in front of an entire camp despite his handicap and proclaim that Jesus loved him. While the boys in the camp had intended their speech for harm, Billy had given control of his speech, as awkward as it was, to God—and God used it to do great things.

One of the most important pilgrim practices of discipleship is speaking wisely. Too often the church has soiled its witness by speaking unwisely—by saying hurtful, untrue, and outright stupid things. Too often we have all hurt our individual witnesses by doing the same. Speaking wisely begins with the way we view the world. God's great gift opens a new way of seeing the world not as a place of violence, mistrust, and conflict but as a place of reconciliation and redemption. When we believe, commit, and embrace this new reality, we see others as they were intended to be—the image of God—and that transforms the way we speak to them.

If the church is going to renew its commitment to discipleship, for many congregations this will begin with the way members speak to each other. For others, it will begin with the way they speak to those in their communities, neighborhoods, or cities. If the church is going to produce true and committed disciples, it must begin to see everyone—from the office supervisor who grates on our nerves to the murderer sitting on death row to the person in enemy uniform—as a person created in the image of God. If we are going to be disciples, our task of transformation will likely begin with our speech. Like the point guard who develops instinct through repeated basketball practice, the faithful congregation will cultivate habits in its own context to make wise speech a daily practice.

As Christians, and as the church, we have a choice to make. To whom do we give control of our tongues? Our speech represents our attitudes and our hearts. With our words, do we proclaim the gospel, do we witness to the message of Jesus, and do we encourage others along this hazardous path of pilgrimage? James says our speech is our rudder, our compass on the journey. It determines how we will travel and what impact we will make. We are on a voyage in a world of strong winds.

Who will be our captain?

9

Witnessing: I Pledge Allegiance . . .

WHO IS WISE AND understanding among you? Show by your good life that your works are done with gentleness born of wisdom. But if you have bitter envy and selfish ambition in your hearts, do not be boastful and false to the truth. Such wisdom does not come down from above, but is earthly, unspiritual, devilish. For where there is envy and selfish ambition, there will also be disorder and wickedness of every kind. But the wisdom from above is first pure, then peaceable, gentle, willing to yield, full of mercy and good fruits, without a trace of partiality or hypocrisy. And a harvest of righteousness is sown in peace for those who make peace.

Those conflicts and disputes among you, where do they come from? Do they not come from your cravings that are at war within you? You want something and do not have it; so you commit murder. And you covet something and cannot obtain it; so you engage in disputes and conflicts. You do not have, because you do not ask. You ask and do not receive, because you ask wrongly, in order to spend what you get on your pleasures. Adulterers! Do you not know that friendship with the world is enmity with God?

Therefore whoever wishes to be a friend of the world becomes an enemy of God. Or do you suppose that it is for nothing

that the scripture says, "God yearns jealously for the spirit that he has made to dwell in us"? But he gives all the more grace; therefore it says, "God opposes the proud, but gives grace to the humble." Submit yourselves therefore to God. Resist the devil, and he will flee from you. Draw near to God, and he will draw near to you. Cleanse your hands, you sinners, and purify your hearts, you double-minded. Lament and mourn and weep. Let your laughter be turned into mourning and your joy into dejection. Humble yourselves before the Lord, and he will exalt you.
(James 3:13—4:10)

Back in the early 1990s, the glory days of contemporary Christian music, there was a popular Christian artist named Ray Boltz. He put out a few tawdry music videos that I remember singing along to in contemporary worship services, and I maintain that every evangelical youth group in America in the '90s performed a skit to his song, "Thank You for Giving to the Lord." (I certainly know I did—more times than I want to count.) Boltz, however, produced one video that struck a deep emotional chord with me and many others. It depicted vivid scenes of martyrdom, people dying for their faith—from martyrs in the early church at the hands of the Roman Empire to martyrs under oppressive regimes in present day. In the song, "I Pledge Allegiance to the Lamb," Boltz sang about turning from the ways of the world and devoting one's whole life to Jesus, giving him everything, placing all trust and loyalty in him above everything else. I pledge allegiance to the Lamb.

This deeply intense and personal and also public and subversive proclamation is the same idea James expresses in James 3 and 4, the pinnacle of his letter. Moving through the pilgrim practices of believing, listening, welcoming, committing, and speaking wisely, this journey now arrives at the culmination of them all—in fact, the essence of discipleship—offering God complete devotion and living as a faithful witness. In fact, I hesitated to title this chapter as I did and thus label witnessing as one practice among others. Christians are to witness as a distinctive practice, but witnessing also encompasses the other practices and underlies the pilgrim journey. Witnessing is simply what we do as we go about our lives.

Discipleship ultimately means forsaking the patterns of this world and witnessing through word and deed to the "upside-down" kingdom and missional movement of God. As James asserts in this troubling section of his letter, faithful witness requires allegiance to the one for whom we witness. Witnessing for God in Christ necessitates allegiance, and not merely partial devotion or divided loyalty; God wants our *complete* allegiance. James puts it in terms of friendship. He says we all have a choice to make, and we all have to make a choice. We cannot be both friends of the world and friends of God.

Best Friends Forever

The contemporary concept of friendship has lost the impact of its original meaning. As people living in the information age, we often use the term "friend" to describe more distant and casual relationships—Facebook friends, Twitter followers, coworkers to whom we barely speak, or friends from various social groups—who are sometimes nothing more than acquaintances. (I have Facebook "friends" I've never even met!) When James used the term "friend" in the first century, however, he meant one of the most faithful and intimate relationships. In Hellenistic culture, friendship was regarded as one of the highest and closest relationships. It was an intense unity, described as "one soul" by Greek philosopher Euripides, "another self" by Cicero, "sharing all things in common" by Aristotle, "and seeing things the same way" by Plato.[1] These images of friendship shape James's usage in James 4. A friend was someone with whom one shared values, hopes, dreams, and ways of living. It signified a loyalty that few of us find or offer in our friendships today. James explains that God wants that extreme loyalty, that radical allegiance—true friendship. But he proceeds a step further. For him, this allegiance is exclusive. You cannot be double-minded friends of both the world and of God.

This is the problem James saw in the churches to whom he wrote. They were experiencing times of struggle and conflict, disputes and arguments. At the beginning of James 4, he dives into the heart of these disputes and suggests that the roots of these fights are selfish desires, selfish ambition, and envy. The envy and selfishness he describes in 3:14–15 have led to social unrest in the churches, and these notions are things of the "world." Some people want it "my way or the highway." Others are trying to get ahead, to climb some invisible ladder of success, and when they see others ahead of them on that ladder, even fellow church members, they want to bring them down. Jealousy and envy take over, and the fighting ensues.

While the churches claim to be friends of God, they live like they are friends of the world. Within this paradoxical reality, James offers no middle road. James says people can be one or the other. Just as Jesus called his followers to leave behind their occupations, their families, and even their dead (Luke 9:57–62), James warns that true discipleship and faithful witness require undivided loyalty and full commitment to God. This is not an easy message to hear, much less live out!

In order to describe this paradox, James lists many accusations against the churches (4:2). It seems that due to some of the socioeconomic disparities and inequalities mentioned earlier in the letter (see Jas 2), an emphasis on materialism and status has led to envy and jealousy in the congregations. These congregations have become so dependent on material possessions and on acquiring more and more that in verse 3 they pray only to satisfy their own desires (4:3). They have turned God into a mere instrument of material acquisition, a "genie in a bottle," a way of getting the things they want. Envy and selfishness undergird the conflicts and attitudes in these churches, and this is a reality of "the world." In our consumer culture of designer clothing, luxury cars, HDTVs, and smartphones, it is not difficult to find ourselves with the same posture or attitude—the attitude James calls "friendship with the world."

A Whole New World

James does not use the term "world" geographically. He is not calling us to forsake the earth or the suffering of people who inhabit it. For James the term *kosmos*, or "world," represents not an actual place but a way of understanding reality. In 1:27 he urged his readers not to be polluted by the world. It is not a matter of geography but of epistemology and philosophy, a life system at odds with God. It is a way of living without God's presence—a life of temptation, self-centeredness, and violence.[2]

This is an easy trap: by living in "the world" we can try to get our own way, climb the ladder of success, and do what it takes to get what we want. It is easy to allow narcissistic ambition to overtake us and desires of the world such as wealth and power to seduce us into selling our souls to gain the world. Often our identity is derived from what we can acquire or possess—"clothes make the man"—rather than from God's implanted word inside us. We are labeled rich or poor, success or failure, wanted or unloved, leaving us never completely satisfied.

In a memorable scene from his book *Searching for God Knows What*, Donald Miller took a moment to ponder what an alien might think of the human species after observing us for a short time. He imagined the aliens' conversation after the visit.

> Humans, as a species, are constantly, and in every way compar-
> ing themselves to one another. It is their driving influence. It is
> as though something that helped them function and live well has
> gone missing, and they are pining for that missing thing in all
> sorts of odd methods, none of which are working. "You guys," the
> alien would say, "are obsessed. You have to wear a certain kind of
> clothes, drive a certain car, speak a certain way, live in a certain
> neighborhood, whatever, all so that you can be higher on an invis-
> ible hierarchy. Who told you there was anything wrong with you
> in the first place?"[3]

Who told you there was anything wrong with you in the first place?
Often we are duped into believing there is something wrong with us if we do not have a six-figure salary, become the perfect parent, achieve straight As, or make everyone like us; we forget that a friendship with a world that presupposes these conditions is no friendship at all. Christians have a habit of letting the world tell us there is something wrong if we do not live up to certain standards of success—money, power, race, national-ity, popularity—rather than claiming our identity in the Christ who says none of that other stuff matters.

A Godly Friendship

James echoes the prominent themes from the beginning of James 2, liv-ing in this new kingdom of God and the social implications of this new allegiance. In James 2 he spoke of the openness and radical welcome of the "upside-down" kingdom life, but he also warned the churches about intermingling with the empire. Creating alliances with the power struc-tures may lead to convenient fixes and assured security, but that is friend-ship with the world. James cautions his readers that these relationships can only lead to compromises in the distinctive Christian witness and a breach in full allegiance to God.

This time, again, James minces no words; he does not tiptoe around the issue. He asks, "You adulterers, do you not know that friendship with the world is hatred toward God?" (4:4). James connects being friends with the world with living according to the earthly wisdom he mentioned in James 3. This wisdom, doing things for myself, doing things so I can get my way or get ahead, leads to disorder and evil. But the wisdom of God that comes from being friends of God leads to peace, mercy, and good works. The churches James was writing to had been seduced by the wisdom of the world. It fed their selfish desires but led to a world where God was absent, where sin became a habit, and where lives were torn apart.

There is no room for riding the fence here. As Jesus says in the Sermon on the Mount, you cannot serve two masters; you must cling to one or the other (Matt 6:24). Christians must turn from our old way of life and pledge our sole allegiance to God alone; only then can we truly witness.

In our society, many things compete for our allegiance. Sometimes we pledge allegiance to our family name, to jobs, to possessions, to country, to ourselves. But James says that when we become a Christian, we pledge allegiance to God, and that declaration trumps all others. Again, Bonhoeffer helpfully described discipleship as "allegiance to the person of Jesus Christ," a confession that places us under his cross.[4] We become citizens of heaven (Phil 3:20), and that citizenship is not restricted to a heavenly existence after death. Rather, at our baptism, our earthly citizenship transforms into full citizenship in the kingdom of God. While nations allow "dual-citizenship" identities, such is not the case with God. My passport and requirement to pay taxes indicate a United States citizenship, but my citizenship in the upside-down kingdom of God and inclusion into the Body of Christ form my thoughts and actions. When my government asks me to kill others in the name of country, when my job asks me to sacrifice time from church and family, when my selfish desires compel me to do what I can to succeed at the expense of others, I must first remember my true allegiance is not to nation, job, or self.

When a work ethic of individual achievement, creeds such as the Pledge of Allegiance, and civic holidays such as Memorial Day work to form us into "good citizens" of the empires of consumerism and nationalism, the practices of the church enable us to witness by telling the world another story. By gathering to worship and orienting our lives according to the church calendar rather than national celebrations, by singing hymns or reciting affirmations of faith in God, and by celebrating community over individual achievement through rituals like Communion and baptism, the church embodies the narrative of Scripture in its daily life. It lives according to a different narrative than the story the world gives us. Practices shape and affirm our allegiance to God at the same time, and they mold Christian imagination in a way that crafts "a character shaped in the image of God."[5] Witnessing to a world that is watching, that is looking for something different and somewhere to place its hope, requires granting full allegiance to God. God wants it all.

A great illustration of submitting fully to God comes from sixteenth-century Russia. Czar Ivan IV, later called Ivan the Terrible, was trying his best to live into his nickname.[6] A "pious tyrant," Ivan ravaged his own land and ruthlessly murdered his perceived enemies, while continually seeking the guidance of the local bishop, in Orthodoxy called a "metropolitan." After ridding himself of one spiritual guide after another, the czar chose a childhood friend, Metropolitan Philip, who had recently retired. Reports convey that Philip "wept at the compulsion that dragged him from his retirement," and knowing the danger of the task before him, "went forth with the spirit of a hero and a martyr." Ignoring the warnings of other bishops, Philip began to openly rebuke Ivan's cruel exploits. The bishop even refused communion to the czar when he came to church with his security forces. Upon this embarrassment, Ivan threatened his friend's life. Philip replied, "I am a stranger and a pilgrim upon earth, as all my fathers were, and I am ready to suffer for the truth. Where would be my faith if I kept silent?" Fully understanding the perils of pledging allegiance to God over state, friendship, and personal safety, Philip was quickly imprisoned, and after receiving the gift of a severed head of a family member, was strangled to death upon Ivan's order.

Philip understood that his pilgrimage might entail his death. He knew it was "all or nothing" and chose God anyway. The pilgrim Way is a narrow one-way path, and this is a difficult message for disciples who have been shaped by commitments to nation, job security, family, or personal ambition. Witnessing, however, requires a life that looks different from that of the "world." It requires being a part of an alternative society that lives according to a different set of ethics shaped by the guidance of scripture and Spirit, cultivated through practices, and pointing toward primal allegiance to God.

It calls us to live life according to the kingdom of God—a different way of living, a different set of ethics, a completely different reality. That is, it calls us to live in a way where the number one rule is to love your neighbor as yourself. As Christians, we operate in a different reality where God offers us good gifts and wisdom, and calls us as believers to live lives that bless others.

Devoting our time to help AIDS victims who are isolated from society.

Doing nice things for the person at work who is always putting us down.

Looking beyond national borders and caring for the resident aliens in our midst, regardless of their immigration status.

Cultivating a relationship with the person who is searching for meaning and asking questions, wanting to know if there is something more out there.

This is the place where we discover our identity. Witnessing is our way of life.

I pledge allegiance to the Lamb.

The Wacky Wisdom of God

This new identity, given to us at our baptism in the trinitarian name of Father, Son, and Holy Spirit spoken over us in this life-changing event (2:7, see chapter 6, "Welcoming"), makes a difference in all areas of life. The wisdom of God opens imaginative new opportunities. In the wisdom of the world, with issues like abortion, for example, we are only offered two choices—advocating for pro-choice or pro-life. The wisdom of the world offers privatized approaches to morality, disregarding the story of Scripture and the witness of the church and therefore confining lines of discourse and ways of responding strictly to the language of individual rights or legal action. But in the wisdom of God, as friends of God, we operate according to another reality, ruled by the command to love neighbor as self. In the world as friends of God we look for ways to witness, to show love as Jesus did. Greg Boyd effectively illustrates the distinctive witness of the wisdom of God in a story from his congregation.[7]

Dorothy was a middle-aged divorced woman who lived alone. One day Becky, a high school senior who had recently been accepted at a local college with aspirations of vet school, showed up at her front door. Dorothy could tell she had been crying. Dorothy had met Becky several years ago, and they had formed a strong relationship.

Shaking and tearful, Becky whispered that she was pregnant. She was afraid to tell her parents, knowing they would kick her out of the house. She was worried that keeping the baby might ruin her dreams of attending college and veterinarian school. She told Dorothy she planned to have an abortion.

Dorothy explained sincerely that if she proceeded with the abortion plans, she would help her in her recovery from the abortion. Believing, however, that it was best to refrain from a violent solution and to carry the pregnancy through, Dorothy encouraged Becky to think seriously about her plans. She offered to do whatever it took to make that an option. Dorothy offered a place to stay and her financial and emotional support. Ultimately, Becky decided not to have an abortion, although her parents did force her to move out of the house. Dorothy opened up her home and cared for Becky and her new daughter. She even took out a second mortgage on her house to help support her financially, and she worked two jobs to help put Becky through vet school. Dorothy became the godmother of Becky's baby, and together they raised the child.

Dorothy was willing to sacrifice herself in order to help Becky. Her decision had nothing to do with political party affiliation, legalized rights to life or rights to choose, or scientific evidence about when life begins. It had nothing to do with these traditional options and categories assigned to us for moral discernment—the wisdom of the world.

The wisdom of God transforms the church into a peculiar people. We are a people not confined to worldly wisdom and traditional social and political paths of transformation. Instead, we are a people who find creative ways to join God's mission in the world, to be the church. The church seeks subversive practices, witnessing to the strange and radical wisdom of God.

Rather than lobbying for state-run health care, for example, there are thousands of Christian doctors in the United States who could afford to launch free clinics out of churches.

Rather than arguing to overturn *Roe v. Wade* on the world's terms of individual rights, churches could encourage members to care for unwed mothers or adopt unwanted babies rather than accommodate the narcissistic desire to have children of one's "own."

Rather than only sending contributions to humanitarian organizations, churches could open up housing for misplaced refugees or immigrants persecuted within our own borders.

Rather than talking about ethereal or personal notions of peace or protesting war on a street corner, churches could teach their youth that Christians are a people of nonviolence, care for soldiers having difficulty leaving the military, or lead groups on peacekeeping trips to war-ravaged countries.

Rather than spending millions of dollars on state-of-the-art recreation facilities or grandiose sanctuaries in efforts to attract newcomers and acquiesce to members, churches could give that money to help their communities or plant churches and reach out to newcomers through authentic fellowship and radical hospitality.

When we pledge allegiance to the Lamb, we are offering commitment to the Lamb, to the one who operates outside the worldly structures, to the one who came not as a political leader, a violent conqueror, a successful businessman, or a popular celebrity. He came in the image of God. He came as a sacrifice, "a lamb to the slaughter"—and calls us to do the same: to find creative and imaginative ways to empty ourselves in witness to the world. Jesus is called the Lamb of God because, like lambs in the Jewish sacrifices, he gave up himself in life and in death on the cross so that we could have a new way of life, so that we could be set free from guilt and sin. When we pledge our allegiance to the Lamb, we are committing to live in the same way—turning from old patterns of life, putting others first even when we do not want to, not fighting back even when someone tries to hurt us, looking out for those neglected by our society even when it is not the easy thing to do. We are committing to living in a way where laying down our lives for a friend, or an enemy, is the ultimate act of love. We are committing to living a life, in Yoder's famous words, "of which the cross is the culmination," and thus demonstrating to the world a new way of life, a new reality possible in Christ.[8]

This is not a way that makes sense to the world. The wisdom of God (much like the thought of God dying on a cross) is foolishness to the world. It is not a pattern for self-help, material gain, or vocational success—in fact, it may mean many of us lose our jobs, live poorly, and experience suffering. It is a pilgrimage of carrying our crosses. That's what it means to pledge allegiance to the Lamb.

The Sacrifice of Witness

After detailing the difference between friendship with God and friendship with the world, James explains what it takes to offer friendship to God alone. Draw near to God, clean your hands, purify your hearts, mourn and weep, humble yourselves before God (4:8–10). These are images of repentance, of a people truly sorry for the wrong they do, truly seeking a new way of living. James indicates that witnessing begins first with repentance, echoing Jesus' opening words in Mark, "The kingdom of God is at hand. Repent and believe the good news" (Mark 1:15). The term "repentance" means turning from one way toward another—turning from the envy and selfishness of the world and turning to the sacrifice and peace in the wisdom of God.

It means a continual renewal of our friendship with God. It means an everyday commitment to God. It means pledging to listen, speak wisely, and witness to this friendship in every part of your life. Because a right relationship with God necessitates right relationships with others, friendship with God means committing to one another, pledging to become part of a radical community, being a missional church that lives by a different truth than that of the world. We need to be a community that proclaims the truth—the kingdom of God is already here, and we are part of it![9] While we continually fail and fall short, God calls us to clean our hands, to repent, to renew our relationship, and to spread the kingdom everywhere we go.

Recalling events in 1964 rural North Carolina at the height of the civil rights movement, Tim Tyson told the story of racial tension in his hometown of Oxford.[10] Tim's father, the town's Methodist pastor, had invited Dr. Samuel Proctor, a leading black preacher, professor, and activist, to speak to his all-white congregation on Race Relations Sunday. The congregation and entire town were furious. The Tysons immediately received opposition, even in the form of death threats. The night before the guest appearance, Tim wrote, his father called a church meeting where the church board angrily demanded a cancellation of the service. "This is going to tear the church apart," they said. Just when Reverend Tyson had nearly heard enough, Miss Amy, a sixty-year-old "old-maid schoolteacher," addressed the board. "When Miss Amy was talking," one member later said, "old Love just come up in my heart." The board decided to allow Dr. Proctor to preach, and his sermon transformed the congregation.

One lay leader, Carl, who had fervently opposed Dr. Proctor's visit and had made his thoughts well known to Reverend Tyson, came into Tyson's office that next week. Tim described the encounter after a later interview with Carl:

> [Carl explained,] "I went to see one of my merchants this morning and he said, 'Carl, you go up there to that church, don't you? Are you going to support your preacher having that nigger up there?' And I said, 'Yeah, I am going to support him.' And that merchant told me to get the hell out of his store and never to set foot in there again." Carl looked at my father and smiled through his tears. "Preacher," he said, "I've heard all my life about witnessing, but until this morning I didn't know a damn thing about it."

To whom do we pledge our allegiance? We can't ride the fence on this one. We can't jump back and forth to please everyone. Being a disciple means a total commitment—to God, to the church, and to God's mission in the world.

God is asking us to live as a lamb, as a sacrifice for others.

God is asking us to forsake selfish desires and love others as God loves us.

God is asking us to live in such a way that others know God by witnessing our life together.

God is asking for it all.

I pledge allegiance.

10

Caring: If We Are with Them

COME NOW, YOU WHO say, "Today or tomorrow we will go to such and such a town and spend a year there, doing business and making money." Yet you do not even know what tomorrow will bring. What is your life? For you are a mist that appears for a little while and then vanishes. Instead you ought to say, "If the Lord wishes, we will live and do this or that." As it is, you boast in your arrogance; all such boasting is evil. Anyone, then, who knows the right thing to do and fails to do it, commits sin.

Come now, you rich people, weep and wail for the miseries that are coming to you. Your riches have rotted, and your clothes are moth-eaten. Your gold and silver have rusted, and their rust will be evidence against you, and it will eat your flesh like fire. You have laid up treasure for the last days. Listen! The wages of the laborers who mowed your fields, which you kept back by fraud, cry out, and the cries of the harvesters have reached the ears of the Lord of hosts. You have lived on the earth in luxury and in pleasure; you have fattened your hearts in a day of slaughter. You have condemned and murdered the righteous one, who does not resist you. (James 4:13—5:6)

Our culture is deeply shaped and formed by images. Imagery suggests what we should want, what we don't like, what we believe, and who we are. Advertisers certainly understand this and drench in us images of their products from billboards to magazines to television commercials. Figures of golden arches, swooshes, or round mouse ears automatically evoke thoughts of certain corporations. I am a sucker for scenes of sandy beaches, crystal-blue oceans, and palm trees. You could easily influence me to buy whatever product you are selling if you depict people in your ad having fun on a sunny beach! Images have such power because they linger—our mental apparatus is configured to remember imagery. Sometimes this is good, and sometimes it's bad. Images from movies like *Jaws* cause me to think twice before entering the ocean, while images from horror films like *Halloween* remind me never to run up the stairs alone when I'm being chased by a knife-wielding serial killer.

On a serious note, however, we must acknowledge the influence imagery has on us. Memories of scenes from our childhood inform us of who we are. Images of my grandmothers baking biscuits for a family meal or my parents waking me early to leave for our summer vacation remind me that I am someone who is loved and cared for. Images of my youth minister staying late to talk with me after a meeting or the smiles of congregants when they glean a new insight from a piece of Scripture solidify the centrality of faith in my life and remind me that I am called to God's mission through the church. These are important aspects of who I am and who I want to be.

Images help form our identities. A major encyclopedia of religious terms begins its definition of "image" by referencing the philosopher Plato. In the fifth century BCE, Plato wrote in his *Republic*, "I strain after images," defining philosophy as the search for images that give an adequate picture of the world in which humans live, relate to one another, struggle for sustenance, and face inevitable death. No one image can offer the "big picture," but a repertoire of images helps shape the world and the way people see it.[1] In other words, images provide vision, and in this way images inspire *imagination*. This is not purely an etymological connection; it denotes the power of Scripture. By depicting explicit, subtle, graphic, poetic, and memorable images, the Bible shapes the worldview of those who read it and in this way helps to shape their identity.

James is a master of imagery. Throughout his letter he uses images to offer readers a way of seeing the world, seeing humanity, and, most important, seeing a vision of discipleship. James inspires the imagination toward a way of understanding what it means to be a disciple. In the same way modern authors such as Annie Dillard or Elie Wiesel craft harrowingly beautiful images that cannot help but linger with us for the rest of our lives, James understood this power and fashioned imagery to narrate stories throughout his letter, edifying and shaping the identities of the churches to which he was writing into a people who listen to the word within and do what it says.

I have noted many important images from James in these chapters and the implications they have for the pilgrimage of discipleship. Near the end of his sermon-letter, James saves some of his most potent images for last. In many cases, he shares these stories to shape his readers by telling us who we are not called to be as followers of Christ, and in this passage he does it once again. Like scenes from the most gruesome horror movie, or characters from a Stephen King novel, James casts a raw, vivid portrait in these verses as a warning about the importance of economic ethics for the Christian life. Here James offers two stories of misplaced values to guide us toward full reliance on God and to stress our part in God's mission.

More Money, More Problems

"Let us go to such and such a place and do business and make money." This statement seems commonplace and harmless enough, yet James does not let it go. Why does it strike such a nerve? Like Jesus in the Jerusalem temple, he expresses utter disgust with the injustice he witnesses. With dual "Come now" introductions, James responds to two types of economic sin. A theme developed consistently throughout the letter (remember especially 1:9–11 and 2:1–8), economic ethics is once again granted priority as a key aspect of discipleship. Today, as Christians formed by a system of free-market capitalism, we tend to understand issues of money and personal wealth as an intensely private matter. James asserts, however, that finances are a matter for the entire community—a public moral issue of discipleship. These words strike James as careless because the businessmen assume they are in control. Whether it is a sense of financial entitlement or mere naiveté, these business dealers perfectly embody the "wisdom of the world" (3:15) rather than being "rich in faith" (2:5).

With his first image, James describes business people who appear to take their wealth and prosperity for granted—as a work of their own doing. Theirs is a life of consumption, competition, and profit. Like the Hebrew wisdom teachers (see Prov 27:1; Ps 37:2; Job 14:1–2), James warns that their life is but a mist and they have grossly misplaced their priorities. He foreshadows the theme of God-dependence that becomes more profound in the next chapter. They are chasing after the ephemeral, not the things that last or the things that truly matter. By prioritizing their lives around material consumption, these business dealers have placed their identity in their wealth.

James's illustration moves us to ask what difference our economics make for the life of discipleship. James's image indicates that "personal" financial matters are a public issue for the church that seeks to be missional. He points us toward a different view of reality, to a new way of seeing "how things really are" (see ch. 4, "Believing"). How do we live in the reality of a God who is the ultimate giver of good gifts (1:17)? Beyond handing out a few dollars to the homeless person on the street, our identity as disciples of a Christ who was homeless, who presumably owned nothing of his own, who shared all he had, indicates that we place too much value in our own family and personal finances.

In fact, the description in Acts of the first-century church, a community possibly led by James, questions the validity of private finances at all (Acts 2:42–47; 4:32–34). Money could not be a determinant of personal identity because no one had money or an income of her or his own but shared it with the entire church community. All economics were communal economics. In such a time as now, with economic disparity at an all-time high, with racing economic growth in some areas of the world and devastating poverty in others, perhaps it is time to rethink the way Christians envision economics. In our capitalist system, churches are not likely to return to the early church communal model, but congregations ought to consider the implications of the lifestyles they choose. Maybe this is not only a model for the "new monastic communities" springing up all over the nation and is not just a description of the early church in a completely foreign time and context. Maybe it is actually the ideal toward which we should move in our congregations today. Again, perhaps it is more prescription than mere description.

In the least, it means we should re-envision the way we talk about money in the church—and not only during stewardship month! When I was a child my pastor used to joke that "Stewardship Month" brought the worst worship attendance of the year. Mostly this is because people do not like to talk about or even hear about money in public. But perhaps this also has to do with church leaders not challenging churches enough! Perhaps pleading for a 10 percent tithe is the starting point and not the goal. Stewardship (and economic ethics) goes way beyond 10 percent of one's income; it matters for the way Christians spend our resources and the way we think about money in the first place. Maybe the way I spend my income and you spend yours should become a matter for the entire church body and not an individual decision. These are ideas that may seem impractical, but for a culture so consumed with financial accumulation, they might be the only way of moving beyond a personal identity located in economic status.

James's message should also challenge churches who have co-opted the business and market model of the world. Some churches and contemporary ministries are run like corporations with senior pastors as the CEOs and millions of dollars raised to build larger buildings or extravagant recreation facilities for member use while the homeless sleep on benches down the street. We think state-of-the-art worship technology (the very phrase causes me to cringe) and elegant education buildings lead to church growth, and in some ways they may, but I wonder if such things lead to faithful witness and committed discipleship!

Do the Right Thing

Verse 17 is also worth noting, specifically for understanding the importance and serious business of pilgrim practices. Most churchgoers have heard sins divided into the categories of sins of commission and sins of omission. I remember in youth group being told the "Thou shalt nots." Thou shalt not have sex before marriage, thou shalt not drink, or cuss, or chew, or go with girls that do! For many, discipleship is much more about the things you can't do rather than the things God calls you to do. For some, this makes Christianity a life of negation, and for others it offers a sense of contentment—as long as I'm not doing those bad things, I am doing all I need to do. This verse, however, suggests that anyone who knows the right thing to do but does not do it sins just as well. James says there is always more good you can do! Sin is not confined to lewd acts. Sin is not limited to murder, thievery, and lies but expanded to the one who does not care for the marginalized "least of these" (1:27), who sees the person in need and does not help (2:16), who does not make peace (3:18), who does not submit his whole self to God (4:7). I cannot read this verse without thinking about those people begging on the sidewalk whom I have pretended not to hear hear, those opportunities to share an encouraging word when I did not feel like having a long conversation, or those times when I could have admitted my mistake but let pride keep me from begging forgiveness.

For those of us who become complacent with the status quo, who forget our dependence on God, who have faith but no works to show for it, James tells us that true discipleship is not only about not doing certain bad things but also about doing good things. In this case, following Christ is about *doing something* with our money for good—being "doers" of the word! Money is not only a thing with which to be cautious but is also an obligation to do good. In short, discipleship is a life of practice—not just avoiding the bad actions, habits, and practices in life but seeking out the pilgrim practices that shape and form us into the Body of Christ.

Flesh-eating Wealth

In his ultimate example of people who know the right thing to do but refuse to do it—and his sharpest critique of the entire letter—James submits a frightening, apocalyptic image of economics gone awry. In the manner of Hebrew prophets like Amos and Isaiah, James paints a horrifying image and tells a vivid story of greed, oppression, violence, and retribution. Owners do not pay their laborers, gold and silver turn into rust, and clothes are ridden with moths. As intense as this scene is, the context behind such scenarios was not foreign to James's readers. In her study of wealth and poverty in the New Testament, Sandra Wheeler suggests that the communities to whom James was writing likely included people who suffered in such economic circumstances. James was writing to people who were suffering like the peasants in his story.[2] In this period in the Mediterranean region, rural wealth had become heavily concentrated in the hands of a few. Smaller farmers were squeezed out of business and forced to become day laborers on the plantations of the rich. These wealthy landowners had complete control over the economic and legal systems, leaving the poor with no outlet for relief. They could deny pay and victimize their wage-laborers with little fear of retribution, and they did.[3] James's readers were the ones suffering oppression, losing their lands, their money, and all control, and gradually losing all hope.

This scene is similar to that of many Americans today. According to the National Priorities Project, a laborer in the United States in the year 2000 making minimum wage earned only about $10,700 a year—below the poverty level. With no minimum wage, small farmers sometimes make even less. In total, 35 million people live below the poverty line, and that is just in the U.S. Across the globe, more than 1 billion people—1 out of every 6—live below the international poverty line.[4] We are not that removed from the same context as James's original readers, and we might ask ourselves which characters we would be in this drama. Perhaps it is time we heeded the calls of liberation theologians to love everyone but still grant a "preferential option for the poor," as it seems clear in Scripture that God does.[5]

To compound the already systemic problems in this scene, the wealthy landowners were robbing the workers of their daily wage. Leviticus 19 specifically prohibits the withholding of wages—the most obvious case of not doing the right thing. The wealthy were once again placing their identity in the fleeting pleasures of the world and oppressing their workers, and James had enough. In language once again similar to Jesus' teachings in Luke 6:24–25—"But woe to you who are rich, for you have already received your comfort. Woe to you who are well fed now, for you will go hungry"—James does not as much warn the rich as he prophesies their demise: riches rotting, moths eating clothes, gold turning to rust and "eating your flesh like fire." Despite such terrifying and cruel threats, James's choice of imagery has important implications.

The interesting thing about this statement is that gold and silver do not actually rust. So why did James say this? What did he mean? Rather than simply making an ancient metallurgical mistake, it seems James was once again trying to make a particular point. The "evidence/witness against you" of the rusty gold and silver is an indictment of James 4:17—a case of not doing good. Wheeler notes that rust is a symbol of inactivity, of uselessness. The inactivity of the rich man's money—"laid up treasure for the last days"—means the rich owner was not "doing good" with his money, not offering alms to the poor through the church or synagogue, as was the duty of every member. The rust signifies that the owner hoarded the wealth for himself rather than sharing it with the poor, and this sign of ultimate greed and misplaced identity would eventually destroy him; it would eat away his flesh.[6]

One thing is certain. James is not cryptic or ambiguous when it comes to his views on money; he simply and explicitly views it as a hindrance to one's discipleship. Arthur Simon, the founder of the humanitarian organization Bread for the World, sums up this point, saying that affluence "turns our hearts towards fleeting satisfactions and away from God."[7] Wealth is a barrier to undivided allegiance to God. "It is easier for a camel to go through the eye of a needle," illustrates Jesus, "than for someone who is rich to enter the kingdom of God" (Mark 10:25), and James fully concurs.

Activist and author Shane Claiborne tells the story of his unusual experience on Wall Street.[8] He had heard of a recent New York City ordinance forbidding the homeless to sleep in certain parts of the city where the homeless often gathered. Thinking the law to be egregious, he was intentionally arrested for sleeping in a New York City park and subsequently won an appeal for wrongful arrest. Wanting to give the lawsuit funds back to the homeless of the city, he and some friends went to Wall Street dressed as business executives, homeless people, and everyone in between. They sent word to all shelters to encourage their homeless to join them on Wall Street. One person in the group climbed the steps to the stock exchange and blew a horn symbolizing the Hebrew Jubilee—the celebration occurring every fifty years when all debts were forgiven (Lev 25).[9] With the blow of the horn, Shane and his friends threw thousands of dollars of coins and small bills into the air. In the place that symbolizes the economic disparity of our time, Shane's group, for a few brief moments, overturned the economic wisdom of the world. Greed and competition were turned into sharing. Allegiance to the economic systems of our country was turned into allegiance to the ways of God.

Radical Nonresistance

Verse 6 offers the final image of this section, that of the "murdered righteous one, who does not resist you." Scholars are divided about who this righteous one is and how he does not resist. For some, the reference is clearly about Jesus, an innocent one who was killed and did not resist the governing authorities. For others, it seems like an allusion to James himself, perhaps added by a late redactor of the book. (Tradition dictates that James, the brother of Jesus and leader of the Jerusalem congregation, followed his brother in death in 62 CE, dying as a willful martyr for the sake of the church he worked so hard to uphold.[10]) While these allusions may certainly be implied through this verse, it most directly refers to the workers, the wage-laborers and Christ-followers who made up the churches reading James's letter. These righteous ones were being killed—both through economic oppression and through outright violence—and were dying as martyrs for their faith.

The odd thing for modern readers is that James does not urge his original readers to stand up in resistance. He does not command them to organize, gather weapons, and fight back. Instead, he commends them because they do not resist. The term James chooses for "resist," *antitassio* in Greek, is a literal term of war, meaning "to battle against."[11] It is a term fraught with violence. James is telling his readers that the righteous do not battle their oppressors. They do not go to war. In this short sentence, James is calling these oppressed and beaten laborers—these committed church members who are slowly dying at the hands of the wealthy—to follow their Savior in the path of nonviolence.

In short, nonviolence is another constitutive aspect of discipleship. New Testament scholar Richard Hays commented, "If our reasons for choosing non-violence are shaped by the New Testament witness, we act in simple obedience to the God who willed that His own Son should give himself up to death on a cross . . . . That is the life of discipleship to which the New Testament repeatedly calls us."[12] If the church is to truly be a community of disciples who attempt to imitate Jesus, if we are going to be a witness to the world that another Way is possible, that another reality is already here, then we are going to have to do so by no longer conforming to the violent ways of the world. Too often our churches enable violence by not speaking loudly enough against war, nuclear weapons, and retaliation. Too often our churches seem to forget these clear images from the New Testament, from books like James, and do not allow them to shape our identities into communities of nonviolence. We allow other forces like patriotism, insecurity, and pragmatism to co-opt our true calling and shape us in ways incongruent with the gospel story. "James' call to active, non-violent resistance," noted commentator Christopher Church, "goes hand in hand with the pacifism familiar in the sayings of Jesus. . . . If we see things as God sees them, if our hearts are stirred as God's is, we will take our rightful place in the struggle against oppression but should do so only by using God's non-violent means."[13]

It may seem that poverty and violence, the two topics of this chapter, are separate issues. Many scholars and ministers, however, have noted an interconnection between the two, most prominently Martin Luther King Jr., who famously said that war was the enemy of the poor. In several of his sermons and speeches, King claimed that as long as America invested its money and human power in military conflict, it would never invest the funds or energies in rehabilitating the poor. With a government that still today appropriates a large segment of its budget to military spending, it seems not much has changed in forty years. Poverty and war will always be linked in opposition to the Gospel, especially in "a society gone mad on war."[14]

The vision James paints in these verses strikes up against everything contemporary American society stands for and teaches us. We are formed by the wisdom of country and nationalism that trains us to be good citizens who will fight for the American way of life and national security. We offer Christian support to the violence used to protect this way of life. Father George Zabelka, Air Force chaplain during World War II who blessed the men and mission that dropped atomic bombs on two Japanese cities, noted the disconnect between the national calling to defend, resist, and strike back and the Christian call to love neighbors and enemies alike in a speech on the fortieth anniversary of the atomic bombings: "I sang 'Praise the Lord' and passed out ammunition. As Catholic chaplain for the 509th Composite Group, I was the final channel that communicated this fraudulent image of Christ to the crews of the Enola Gay and the Boxcar [*sic*]. All I can say today is that I was wrong," he confessed. "Today the world is on the brink of ruin because the Church refuses to be the Church, because we Christians have been deceiving ourselves and the non-Christian world about the truth of Christ. There is no way to follow Christ, to love as Christ loved, and simultaneously to kill other people."[15]

This is a calling the church in America needs to take seriously. More years of my life have witnessed our nation engaged in military conflict than years that have not. Living in a nation that has perpetually engaged in war for the better part of the past century, Christian pilgrims have an urgent calling to begin dealing with issues that matter. If the missional church is going to make a real difference in this world, we must begin by not worrying as much about being culturally "relevant," appeasing national sentiments, or growing our church roles, and begin embodying the key dimensions of discipleship. And why not start with one of the most radical and central witnesses of all, that of nonviolent peacemaking?

James's statements about economics and nonviolence imply a certain degree of allegiance and commitment in churches. James casts a radical vision for a new social order within the church and witness to the world. Accumulation of wealth and submission to the ways of violence are mere wisdom of the world and not of God. This type of ethical vision does not sit well with people, especially those with power and influence or those at ease with the status quo. While James advocates for a new morality defined by good works, we see that it is impossible without faith. This new movement begins with radical belief in and dependence on God.

Being the Presence

In the end, despite the harsh imagery and urgent call to action, this message is one of hope. Like the wages in Deuteronomy 24:15, the unpaid wages of these laborers cry out and reach the ears of God. Despite the oppression and murder, God is not absent but promises redemption. Judgment and retaliation are not pilgrim responsibilities. War and revenge are not the calling of disciples. But faithfulness, trust, and the doing of good certainly are.

When I was a child and we had just moved into a new house, I was scared to go to sleep in my room by myself. Every night I would ask my mom to sit in my room until I fell asleep. She started out directly beside my bed, but as the nights went on she gradually moved closer to the door, then to the hallway, and finally out of sight. But during those dark nights, she made me feel safe. Her presence was all that mattered to a scared child who felt alone in the dark. Her presence was enough.

For those in the darkness of poverty, oppression, or war, God's presence can be enough. God's presence overcomes the darkness and takes away fear. God promises to be there, but God calls the church now to be that presence in the dark: that is, as the Body of Christ to be the presence of Christ to those in need. Several years ago, Bono, lead singer from the band U2 and influential advocate in the struggle against global poverty, gave a sermon at the National Prayer Breakfast.[16] During his message, Bono told of a time in his life when he asked God to bless the work he was doing. A mentor told him to stop asking God to bless what he was doing and get involved with what God is doing, because it's already blessed. "Well," Bono said, "God is with the poor. That is what God is doing. God is in the slums, in the cardboard boxes where the poor play house. God is in the silence of a mother who has infected her child with a virus that will end both of their lives. God is in the cries heard under the rubble of war. God is in the debris of wasted opportunities and lives, and God is with us, if we are with them."

While James's verses serve as a stark warning about the love of money and the dangers of unknowingly placing our identity in worldly measures, it also teaches us about the value of the pilgrim practice of caring. Missional communities are communities of compassion. Sometimes this caring is embodied in witness—intentionally forsaking the wealth of the world in imitation of our homeless Savior. Sometimes this caring is embodied in direct action—standing up for the poor and outcast, as in the story of Shane Claiborne. Sometimes this caring is embodied in non-violence—maintaining a posture of peacemaking when the oppressors are closing in. Sometimes this caring is simply embodied in presence—being the presence of Christ in a world of darkness. Discipleship is necessarily about being out in the world, shouting and showing that another Way is possible, being with those in desperate need of the presence of our God.

Discipleship is about joining God's mission to the most neglected, hated, marginalized, oppressed, and lost. And the good news is that God will be right there with us if we are with them.

11

Praying: The Problem of Independence

BE PATIENT, THEREFORE, BELOVED, *until the coming of the Lord. The farmer waits for the precious crop from the earth, being patient with it until it receives the early and the late rains. You also must be patient. Strengthen your hearts, for the coming of the Lord is near.*

Are any among you suffering? They should pray. Are any cheerful? They should sing songs of praise. Are any among you sick? They should call for the elders of the church and have them pray over them, anointing them with oil in the name of the Lord. The prayer of faith will save the sick, and the Lord will raise them up; and anyone who has committed sins will be forgiven. Therefore confess your sins to one another, and pray for one another, so that you may be healed. The prayer of the righteous is powerful and effective. (James 5:7–8, 13–16)

I am often amused by scenes of prayer in movies. There is a humorous portrayal in the comedy *Meet the Parents* where Greg, played by Ben Stiller, goes home with his fiancée to, of course, meet her parents.[1] One evening before the meal, her family asks Greg to offer the blessing. Nervous and trying to impress them, he begins,

Oh, dear God, thank you. You are such a good God to us. A kind and gentle and accommodating God, and we thank you, oh sweet, sweet Lord of hosts for the smorgasbord you have so aptly laid at our table this day, and each day, by day, day by day, by day. Oh dear Lord three things we pray: to love Thee more dearly, to see Thee more clearly, to follow Thee more nearly, day, by day, by day. Amen."

From the looks on everyone's faces, including Greg's, it's apparent that Greg has not had much experience saying prayers.

While this scene depicts the comedy in extreme forms of prayer, real prayer can be difficult. I don't know how many times I have made a commitment to set aside time to pray every night before bed only to fall asleep as soon as I get out the words, "Dear Lord, thank you . . . ," or set aside time in the morning when I first wake up only to do the same thing. I've tried kneeling, sitting, standing, walking, eating, and exercising, only to get distracted by the thousands of thoughts streaming through my head. Prayer is a difficult practice.

Several years ago there was a popular series of Holiday Inn Express commercials. They would depict a man performing heart surgery or becoming a rodeo clown or an astronaut. When the person he was helping expressed thanks, he told them he was not really a heart surgeon, but he did stay at a Holiday Inn Express the night before. In the ministry world, and especially as a pastor, that is often how I feel. As a minister I am sometimes called on to do things or to speak on issues where I do not feel equipped to lead people. Maybe they are issues with which I have not had personal experience. Or worse, they may be areas in which I feel inadequate or things with which I struggle. I have often felt in many of my sermons or much of my writing that I wrote the messages just as much for myself as for the congregation or readers.

Prayer is one of those topics on which I do not feel adequate to write something worthwhile. It is an area I struggle with possibly the most in my personal spiritual life—not easy for a minister to admit.

Although arriving at this topic toward the end of his sermon-letter, James denotes the essentiality of prayer, and his comments serve as an appropriate conclusion to this guidebook for the pilgrim journey.

Remember God

For most of his letter, James has exhorted his readers with ethical instructions, detailing life together in Christian community. In the final segment
of the letter, he turns to what Christians often view as a more spiritual
idea, the practice of prayer. But for James, even prayer contains significant
ethical implications. His main point in these six verses is that prayer is the
pathway to healing. It was the way out of the inner struggles and disunity
that lay at the heart of the conflicts in these early churches, and it is the
road to the wisdom of God and healing for both individuals and communities today.

He asks two questions in verse 13: "Are any among you suffering?
Are any cheerful?" The two extremes of life. James's interesting answer is
that the response should be the same: remember God. If you are suffering, pray. If you are cheerful, sing praises to God. In any circumstance,
remember God.

Often, people are generally better at one or the other. When life is
happy, some are extremely grateful to God for good fortune, but when
life gets difficult, they blame God and turn away. For others, when things
go wrong, they have no trouble turning to God to ask for a little help. But
when everything is fine, they tend to forget God is there. James, however,
says that in either situation we should turn to God—in times of praise
and times of struggle. Remember the things God has done in good times
and in bad. Stanley Hauerwas suggested, "The kind of memory that truly
shapes and guides a community is the kind that keeps past events in mind
in a way that draws guidance from them for the future."[2] As with the
Hebrews on the meandering journey to Canaan, it is our remembrance of
God's great work in the past that sustains the journey and our anticipation
of the fullness of God that offers hope for the future. Both guide the community in its journey together.

While prayer can be an effective vehicle for remembrance and a path
to guidance for the future, I think Christians today often view prayer as
an obligatory but not very useful approach to situations. We say, "I will
pray for you," and we mean it, but we don't necessarily expect anything
to change. However, James calls people who are suffering to pray as an
active response to their problems. This is not some passive solution; this

is not merely a mechanical obligation. This is a way to effect change, to help people in need, to bring about healing. We are not simply to accept suffering in quiet resignation, just as we are not to let good fortune go by ungratefully, but we are to be proactive in our response, remembering God is with us at all times.

Body and Soul

In the following verses, James writes further on the subject of prayer during suffering, specifically prayer for those who are sick. While churches today place the names of infirmed congregants on prayer lists and pastoral care teams make visits to the hospital, James introduces an idea foreign to many modern churches—anointing with oil (although this is a practice quite familiar in some charismatic congregations).[3] In the ancient Hellenistic world, most Greek physicians swore oaths to the Greek gods of healing and medicine, leaving faithful Christians without many options for medical care.[4] Oil was often used for medicinal purposes and was expected to have some type of healing power. In the Bible, anointing with oil was used for various purposes, such as preparation for death, treatment for wounds, and healing of the sick. While James advocates the use of anointing oil, he assures his readers that despite the inclinations of Roman culture, the oil is not what brings about the healing (5:15). The power is not in the oil; the power is in the prayer. "The prayer of faith will save the sick." When the elders anointed the infirmed person with oil and pronounced a prayer in the name of Jesus, it was the prayer that would bring the healing, not the oil itself.

James is making a strong statement about the connection between the physical and spiritual. Prayer can both heal the physical ailment and forgive sins; physical and spiritual salvation are connected in a way that the church has forgotten over the years. The Enlightenment focus of the seventeenth and eighteenth centuries on science and rationality precipitated a modern dualism between body and soul, between the physical and spiritual.[5] Modern values relegate healing to the realms of science and medicine while situating the church solely within the spiritual vocation of saving souls. This, however, is not the way the early church understood things, which is evident in biblical language. When James says, "The prayer of faith will save the sick . . . ," the word he uses for "save," *sosei* in Greek, is the same one used throughout the New Testament for both spiritual salvation and physical healing.[6] At one point James uses it to intimate a person "being saved" from their sins (2:14; 5:20), and here he uses it in reference to someone being saved from an illness. The word denotes a more holistic understanding of salvation. In the biblical world there was no dichotomy between physical and spiritual salvation; the two were interwoven. Taking care of one's physical needs went hand in hand with taking care of her spiritual needs.

When I served as a chaplain in the hospital, my favorite patient was a young man who suffered from HIV. The nurses and doctors all said he had gone "crazy," that the drugs and disease had damaged his brain, but I enjoyed the time I spent with him. He was always cheerful, always smiling, and always appreciative for any visit. Some days I would enter his room and find it necessary to inform him he needed to wear clothes if I was going to visit. Some days we would look at workout magazines as he explained how he was going to be a professional football player, or we'd peruse motorcycle magazines as he talked about riding across the country on a bike, or we'd read the Bible as he said he was going to start a church.

Every time I visited, he spoke of the time that God had "healed" him. He had been ill a long time, but the previous year, he said, Jesus had healed him. Jesus came to him in a blaze of white light, touched his face, and turned his hair white as snow. He could feel the warmth inside him as the virus left him and Christ came in. He said he had been healed both from his disease and from his sin. He was a new man, and when he left the hospital, he was going to go and sin no more. Despite what the doctors claimed, that his condition was getting worse, he knew Jesus had healed him—body and soul.

His condition did begin to improve and he was able to leave the hospital. I never saw the young man again, but I never forgot his faith that God had healed him, both his physical ailment and his spiritual sins. For him, it seemed, they were one and the same, and I think disciples could learn from this connection when we care both for people's spiritual and physical needs.

Today, when churches neglect the physical needs of people and narrow the church's vision strictly to evangelistic efforts to convert and save souls without caring for the whole person, we are seen as inauthentic, and I believe it does more to damage our communal witness than it does to help it. Churches intent on being missional must take a more holistic approach to salvation and evangelism—understanding this mysterious connection between body and soul and seeking to heal them both. The spiritual healing dimension may seem more important to us in our individualistic and evangelical culture, and it may also take more effort than the physical dimension, but both are needed in our relationships if we are to live out God's calling for the church.

Hope for the Sick

It is also important to note the connection in this culture between sickness and sin, and in this discussion James returns to his theme of social ethics. In verse 15, he says the prayer will both heal the physical ailment and also forgive the person's sins. The same thing is implied in several of Jesus' healings. It was a popular thought in Jewish culture and Greco-Roman philosophy that if a person was sick, it was the result of some sin or wrongdoing in his life. Since sin and sickness were linked so closely, the infirmed were often marginalized in society. Illness had significant social implications in the wisdom of the world. With this anthropological framework, the sick should be sent out of the community so the healthy would not be infected by their actual illness or their sinful lifestyles. A community that included the sick was not a healthy community, physically or spiritually, and the ill were often isolated.

James, however, again calls the church to behave differently, to live according to the wisdom of God. In short, he calls the church to act missionally. The church is to provide intimate care for the sick, to empower them to call on the elders to come and pray for them, to welcome them as part of the life of the community. Churches are to treat a sick person no differently than they would treat their most powerful member. Here James speaks about intentional practices of the church—prayer and anointing— that should include those who are ill within the fellowship of community.

As you read this, you may be thinking, well at least we do a better job today. We do not isolate and exile those who are sick. We do not believe a person's illness is the result of something she did wrong. But before patting ourselves on the back, let us consider how the church treats people who suffer from certain diseases like HIV/AIDS. We still link certain illnesses with sin, and whether we say it or not, we often have thoughts like, "They brought it on themselves." We still relegate AIDS victims to the margins through statements of condemnation, reticence when it comes to discussions of sexuality in church, explicit homophobic attitudes, and a general lack of support and response to people who suffer from this disease, however they contracted it. AIDS victims are a group of people whom the church has neglected for the past thirty years. Very few churches do anything to bring hope and healing to victims of this devastating illness. The church in America would do well to ask itself, What does it mean to be the Body of Christ when part of that Body is suffering? While we do not always connect every illness with a sinful lifestyle, this attitude still affects the way we treat people who are suffering. We would still do well to heed James's words about healing the whole person, both spiritually and physically.

Bound and Free

In the final verses of this section, James turns his attention once again to the idea of prayer and the theme of dependence on God that has underlined all his ethical discussions. Confess your sins to one another, pray for one another, and this will bring healing. "The prayer of the righteous is powerful and effective." While prayer can bring healing for an individual who is sick, prayer and confession can bring healing for an entire community. It seems that James is calling for a radical form of prayer—offering requests not just before God but before other Christians. Confessing sins not just before God but before other Christians. Bonhoeffer advocated for the practice of mutual confession in his work, *Life Together*. "A man who confesses his sins in the presence of a brother knows that he is no longer alone with himself," he wrote. "He experiences the presence of God in the reality of the other person."[7] The person who confesses now stands in true humble, vulnerable fellowship—not alone, but with other sinners living by God's grace. Bonhoeffer, and James before him, is calling on churches to build radical communities and radical relationships that fully depend on God and each other for support and healing. "The church," noted theologian Miroslav Volf, "is not a club of the perfect, but rather a communion of human beings who confess themselves as sinners and pray: *debita dimitte* [forgive us our debts]."[8] It is a beautiful body with sores and scars—but one Body nonetheless.

For us, this concept runs counter to the way we are taught to live and interact. As I have indicated previously, in our culture we are habituated from the time we are small to be independent; we are taught that depending on someone else is a sign of weakness and failure. We are taught to handle our problems on our own, find our own solutions, and never inconvenience others with our personal issues. "The history of every man is the history of his great and fantastic attempt to help himself," Barth discerned, indicating that this autonomous longing is only a symbol for the real thing we lack.[9] There is no need to rely on anyone else; being independent is a sign of maturity, strength, and wisdom.

This is often the mentality of churches and denominational structures as well. In my own Baptist tradition, we value the freedoms of faith as our core distinctions—religious freedom, local church freedom, and individual spiritual freedom. However, in many ways we are only accommodating to the individualistic impulses of modern American culture, extolling freedom at the expense of community, ecumenism, and the depths of faith. We cherish our heritage of dissension from religious groups that have exerted too much coercive power, but we have done so to an extreme, often permitting claims of freedom to supersede calls to ultimate dependence on each other and on God. Rather than being members of the communal Body of Christ, we are disembodied members who politely greet each other on Sunday mornings. God created us in the image of a Trinitarian relationship of the mutually submissive Father, Son, and Holy Spirit—meaning we were never intended to be independent. The story that forms the church is that my life does not belong to me—it is a gift for others.

Again, Barth is helpful here in offering a truer theological conception of freedom. "He is a free man," he suggested, "when he thinks and decides and acts at peace with God, when his decision is simply and exclusively a repetition of the divine decision."[10] In other words, human freedom given to us by God does not equal modern libertarian notions of independence or autonomy. Rather, true expressions of freedom correspond to obedience before God.[11] As Christians, we operate under a different conception of freedom. We are freed for such radical risks of discipleship as giving our time, money, and even our lives for others because we know death is not the final word and nothing can separate us from the love of Christ. We do not have to live in the same anxious state as others who do not know the redeeming love of Christ. We know we are free to take risks, free to obey, free to live in communion with God and others, free to be bound to a cross.[12]

Dependence on God and trust in God means the interdependence of the community of God. I am not proposing that God does not perform miracles or intervene in human life but suggesting that when we say the church is the Body of Christ, what this signals is that the church cares for its members and cultivates an ethos of interdependence. When we talk about dependence on God what we mean in part is the mutual love and support of the church family lifting up those in need. We come to the aid of those in financial struggles or in loving support of those suffering loss. Dependence is a discipline and a practice that needs to be cultivated, both to free ourselves from the tyrannical allusion of independence and to open ourselves to the loving care of one another. An essential part of cultivating this practice is learning from communities that do dependence well, acknowledging that many of them have been forced to be dependent on God and interdependent as a community because of historical and current oppression, discrimination, or subjugation.[13] For many congregations in America, this might entail learning from communities of ethnic minorities or immigrants. The only way to truly learn utter, naked dependence within the Body of Christ is for churches that have long suffered from independence to join in communion with—*to share life with*—communities that imagine dependence in deeper and more vulnerable ways. This involves more than an occasional "pastor-swap" or fellowship meal, but joining together in risky, vulnerable worship, study, and ministry, as well as the everyday activities of our lives.

Therefore, humans are created to live, worship, interpret Scripture, and practice faith in a community that is responsible before God and in utter need of one another—to tell each other when we mess up, to ask for help, to confess our struggles . . . to admit that I struggle often with prayer because of my urge for independence. I confess that in much of my ecclesial life, and in my personal life, I operate in this same way. I can handle my own problems. I do not need to pray about all this. The reason for this autarchic attitude is that perhaps my faith is not strong enough to think that God could actually change things, heal people, or bring comfort to pain. When I suffer and when I am cheerful, I rely on myself, not God.

And perhaps the same is true for you. Perhaps we do not have enough trust in God . . . or in each other.

The Power of Prayer

As un-pastor-like as it sounds, one reason I find it difficult to trust is that there were times when my prayers went unanswered. As I think back about my patient in the hospital and his faith that God healed him, I have to admit that I do not know if this man was ever healed from HIV. Perhaps he wasn't, despite his faith and despite people praying for him. I can vividly recall times when I prayed diligently for something to happen that never came to fruition. There were times when I pleaded with God to heal someone close and the healing never came. While James says the prayer of the righteous is effective, we have all experienced times when our prayers went unanswered, when the healing never happened. It is hard to be completely dependent on God and others when we have felt that they both let us down in the past.

I admit that I do not have all the answers. I do not understand why loved ones die, hearts break, and people suffer when surrounded by fervent and faithful prayers. I struggle just as much as anyone who may be reading this—and that is part of the mystery of our faith, part of the hazards of pilgrimage.

While I will never know if that devastating virus left my patient's body, I do know that he experienced healing. This may seem like an odd statement. However, I believe a truly Christian and biblical understanding of healing is larger than a cure; true healing is wholeness. This holistic definition of healing seamlessly weaves together the physical and spiritual, taking seriously the Christian convictions and implications of incarnation and resurrection.[14] Illness and sin alike leave people and communities broken. God does not promise always to provide a cure, but God does promise to make us whole once again. In this way, my patient was healed. His broken body and spirit were made whole again. He had a renewed sense of joy and relationship with God. His life and his body were given meaning and purpose. That is where our hope lies. Everyone experiences times of struggle, but James tells us that as the church, as a community of pilgrim disciples, we have each other and we have faith in a God who promises to be there for us through it all.

James is calling pilgrims to have authentic, honest, and vulnerable relationships—with God and with each other. In these relationships, we voice our struggles, ask for help, rely on each other and on the power of God to help and heal, and truly believe that God will heal us somehow.

Everyone is in need of some type of healing. Perhaps you are not physically sick or going through an otherwise extremely difficult time in your life right now. Perhaps you feel like you are doing fine on your own. We all remember and carry with us the scars from times when we were hurt, times we wish things would have turned out differently, times we wish we could go back and do something different, times we have lost people close to us. Even if we feel like we are on cloud nine and nothing can touch us, we all carry with us parts that need to be redeemed, taken away, or healed.

Perhaps in this moment, as you read this, you are experiencing some tough times, you are ill, or you feel desperate. The world is spinning around uncontrollably, and you are overwhelmed, angry, hurt, or hopeless. Perhaps you feel like there is nothing else you can do. For ten chapters this book has focused on being the church for other people and on meeting the needs of others, and the whole time you have been thinking, but what about me? What about *my* needs? One central theme throughout the guidebook of James is that God promises to be with us—in good times and bad. God promises to bring some type of healing, maybe not in the way we expect or hope but in the way we need. God promises God's presence in the darkness if we would just remember and depend on God.

James says the prayer of the righteous can lead to healing. As pilgrims, we are called to be there for each other, and as we work to be more reliable and trustworthy, we work to be more vulnerable and dependent in our pilgrimage together. Prayer is a foundational pilgrim practice not because it achieves the results we want but because it teaches us to be dependent on God and on each other. It teaches us to ask for help, to seek God's healing, and to truly, honestly believe that God is with us.

Afterword

It Takes a Church . . .

> MY BROTHERS AND SISTERS, *if anyone among you wanders from the truth and is brought back by another, you should know that whoever brings back a sinner from wandering will save the sinner's soul from death and will cover a multitude of sins.* (James 5:19–20)

During the first Christian Ethics course I taught to a group of undergraduate students, I spent a significant amount of time explaining how Christian ethical formation was distinct from traditional moral philosophies like Utilitarianism or Kantianism. After a semester of my shaky theological and philosophical meandering, one student raised her hand during our final class and attempted to summarize: "So what you've been teaching us all along is to think Christian *first*."

While I firmly believe that Christian ethics, or discipleship as I like to call it, goes well beyond mere intellectual activity, learning to "think Christian first" is certainly a great place to start. The Apostle Paul had something to say about transformation occurring first within the mind (Rom 12:2). Emmanuel Katongole reminds us that transformation must begin with the renewal of our minds because the Christian story offers a "fresh lens through which to see ourselves, others, and the world." It shapes within us a brand-new identity "by creating a new sense of *we*."[1] What my students were beginning to grasp was that being a disciple on the pilgrim journey of faith means that we do not think first as Democrats,

Republicans, Libertarians, Americans, Southerners, Caucasians, African Americans, Hispanics, Tar Heel fans, or any other identity factor. Instead, Christians turn to the formative stories of Scripture as a guide for the journey, sustained through ecclesial practices of faith, to direct our Way and tell us who we are. "Thinking Christian first" is a great place to begin the journey, but the practices lived out before a world that is watching are what actually make us Christian.

The pilgrim practices described and narrated in this book have a circular dimension. I am reminded of a line from a T. S. Eliot poem: "The end of all our exploring will be to arrive where we started, and know the place for the first time."[2] To end a book on Christian practice with such a thing as prayer may seem about as odd as beginning it with such a thing as belief. While the book of James is filled with exciting ethical exhortations like having compassion, witnessing, and showing hospitality, these "active" practices are bookmarked with the rather worn and tattered categories of prayer and faith. And while these framing elements may come as a surprise, they undoubtedly reveal a great deal about the trajectory of the pilgrim journey. The most important and constant aspect of a life of discipleship is the inextinguishable dependence on something greater than ourselves—found in God and expressed through the Body of Christ in the local church community. The practices of both faith and prayer frame the Christian pilgrimage in a state of dependence on the Spirit of God and on one another. Discipleship both begins and ends, essentially, with trust.

✳ *In short, the first task of discipleship is realizing that you cannot do it on your own.*

James ends his letter in an odd place as well. Rather than the typical personal greetings and benedictions of an ecclesial epistle, James can't resist using his final pen stroke to offer another exhortation about the value of community. Whoever brings back a sinner from wandering covers a multitude of sins. Reflecting the statement in 1 Peter that "love covers a multitude of sins" (4:8), James locates the proper expression of this love within the church community—in the act of bringing the wanderer back into relationship with the fellowship. The practice of love is noticeably absent in the eight practices derived from James's messages on discipleship (the term is only used three times in James—twice regarding love for God and once for the royal law to love neighbor), but I believe this is because love underlines them all. Evident in the ethical actions of a community reaching out to bring those who are prone to wander back into the fold, love is both the source and the manifestation of the pilgrim practices of discipleship.

Love is practiced nowhere more noticeably than in the radical and naked dependence of the disciple. Understanding the book of James as a story of dependence, the pilgrim Way of discipleship is a reminder of both our freedom and our binding as followers of Christ. Ours is a Way of dependence on the gifts of God and guidance of God's Spirit: living in faith "beyond limits," discovering the whisper of the word planted within us, being open to welcoming others into the body of faith, committing body and soul, and seeking wisdom from above and friendship with God. It is also a Way of dependence on each other: offering ourselves to listen to each other and to speak wisely, caring for those in the margins, living as a community of faithful witnesses, and praying earnestly in mutual confession and redemption. Returning to this theme of dependence with the final practice of prayer—arriving, in a way, back at our starting point—opens a refreshing perspective on the pilgrim journey of discipleship, allowing us all to understand it in new ways, or perhaps for the first time. As Eliot's poetic insight makes clear, our exploring is far from over, even when we think we've come to the end.

I hope the practices explored in this journey through James have led you to a clearer and deeper understanding of what it means to be a disciple on the pilgrim journey. Discipleship is not a mere denominational program or congregational study. It is not even primarily about doctrine or action but about being formed by pilgrim practices into a certain identity that can only be discovered in the community we call the church. Through the images and stories of Scripture, and through the faith and practices cultivated in the church, we finally discover our true identity—who we are meant to be. And through the church we then offer a vision of a new reality, a new Way of life, a brand-new creation that the entire world can experience if they accept the call to join us.

It is appropriate to conclude a book on the Christian pilgrimage by remembering Bonhoeffer's description of the pilgrim church community passing, in anticipation, through this world: "At any moment it may receive the signal to move on. Then it will break camp, leaving behind all worldly friends and relatives, and following only the voice of the one who has called it. It leaves the foreign country and moves onward toward its heavenly home."[3] In the end, my prayer is that this will be just the beginning of our mutual journey home. With the urgency of James, I suggest that our work has just begun. The pilgrim Way is fraught with danger and hardship—and as Frodo recalls on his epic journey, going out your door is always dangerous. We will certainly need each other.

Pilgrim Practices Discussion Guide

Chapter 1

1. Why is it important to think of the Christian pilgrimage in communal terms?

2. What are some important practices in the life of your church?

3. What are the implications for reading Scripture as an itinerary rather than a map?

Chapter 2

1. What are the practical implications of the four images of church mentioned in this chapter?

2. How would it affect church ministry to think of church as a road or movement?

3. What other social agendas or institutions do we allow to form our identities? Why are they so appealing?

Chapter 3

1. How does this chapter's description of "missional" resonate with or differ from other descriptions you have read?

2. What does it mean to say that community, or fellowship, is not one practice to be engaged but the context in which all pilgrim practices take place?

3. What would it look like to take Acts 2:42–47 seriously in churches?

Chapter 4

1. Why is faith an important place to begin a study of pilgrim practices? Why do you think James begins his letter with faith?

2. Is it helpful or harmful to think of suffering as making us wiser?

3. How can Christians imagine living in an alternative reality when pain, suffering, and competition are all around us?

Chapter 5

1. In what ways have you experienced God speaking to you?

2. What are ways we can open ourselves to hearing the implanted word within us?

3. What is the difference between seeking God's blessing for us and asking God to bless our work? How might this make us "first fruits"?

Chapter 6

1. What keeps churches from extending a radical welcome to all?

2. What are examples of "Miss Ida" in your context or experience?

3. How might it change the perspective and ministry of your church to view it as one unified Body with sore places and scars, but beautiful nonetheless?

Chapter 7

1. Do you remember your first commitment to a life of discipleship? How do you understand this practice of commitment?

2. How might churches transform evangelism techniques to emphasize a lifelong commitment and practice rather than a single moment of conversion?

3. After reading this chapter, how do you understand the interplay of faith and works?

Chapter 8

1. What does being "created in the image of God" mean to you? How does it affect the way you treat others?

2. What are examples of harmful speech you've witnessed in the church? Examples of wise speech?

3. How can you make speaking wisely a daily practice?

Chapter 9

1. Do you agree that friendship (allegiance) to God must be exclusive in order to give a faithful witness? What does this mean for how Christians interact in the world?

2. What do you make of John Howard Yoder's quote in this chapter, that discipleship is a life "of which the cross is the culmination"? What does that mean?

3. Most churches today do not like to talk about repentance, but how can repentance be the first step in the practice of witnessing?

Chapter 10

1. Do you believe the New Testament calls for an end to personal finance within churches? Is this at all feasible? How might we extend a preferential option for the poor?

2. What are ways the church in America can reclaim the practice of nonviolence that was present in the early church?

3. How can "presence" be a vital ministry in your church?

Chapter 11

1. Do you see independence as a helpful or harmful attitude for discipleship? Why?

2. What would it take to move your congregation to a place where public and communal confession becomes a practice?

3. In what ways do we theologically and ministerially separate the body and the soul? How can we maintain a more holistic approach to healing?

Endnotes

Introduction

1. I will use a lowercase "c" for church throughout this book in an effort to place less stress on the distinction often made between the universal church and local church. In most cases, the usage will be applicable to both contexts, in understanding the local church as both a part and a whole of the Body of Christ.

2. The specific statistics vary depending upon the research group. A Barna Group study found that one-half of Americans in 2008 did not attend church in any form ("New Statistics on Church Attendance and Avoidance," 3 March 2008, http://www.barna.org/barna-update/article/18-congregations/45-new-statistics-on-church-attendance-and-avoidance?q=statistics+church+attendance+avoidance). A 2009 Gallup poll stated that the number of those who self-identify as Christian has dropped from over 90 percent in 1950 to under 80 percent in 2009, while church membership is also down 10 percent ("This Christmas, 78% of Americans identify as Christian," December 24, 2009, http://www.gallup.com/poll/124793/This-Christmas-78-Americans-Identify-Christian.aspx). The American Religion Identification Survey of 2001 discovered that from 1990 to 2001 the percentage of Americans identifying as Christian dropped 15 percent (John Corrigan and Winthrop Hudson, *Religion in America* [Upper Saddle River, NJ: Prentice Hall, 2004] 457). Another recent study affirms church decline since 1950 but refutes some of the more popular statistics, asserting that attendance has leveled off since 1990 (Stanley Presser and Mark Chaves, "Is Religious Service Attendance Declining?" *Journal for the Scientific Study of Religion* 46/3 (2007): 417–23).

3. "America's Religiosity Unique among Industrialized Countries," *Bertelsmann Stiftung Religion Monitor*, 15 December 2009, http://www.bertelsmann-stiftung. de/cps/rde/xchg/SID-61FB6B9E-C76EB5A0/bst_engl/hs.xsl/nachrichten_99201. htm.

4. Quentin Schultz, *Habits of the High-Tech Heart: Living Virtuously in the Information Age* (Grand Rapids: Baker, 2004) 178.

Endnotes

5. This oft-cited claim has received much attention in academic and religious circles in the past twenty years. One of the more seminal sociological works to note the effects of American individualism upon religion twenty-five years ago was Robert Bellah et al., *Habits of the Heart: Individualism and Commitment in American Life* (Berkeley: University of California Press, 1985, 2008).

6. The reader will notice that most of the sources and authors cited in this book are contemporary. While it may be a deficiency in the comprehensive scholarship of the work, I wanted to incorporate the constructive thought primarily of authors whom my readers may find helpful on their journey of discipleship. With a few notable exceptions, most of the works cited in this bibliography are both accessible pieces for theological novices as well as richly theological works for those seeking a more robust account of discipleship.

7. Of course, this is not to say that these are the only eight. Many good authors acknowledge and examine different Christian practices that are important for discipleship. A good place to begin is Dorothy C. Bass, ed., *Practicing Our Faith: A Way of Life for a Searching People* (San Francisco: Josey-Bass, 1997). These authors pull from various sources—other books of Scripture, church traditions, or liturgical practices—to craft these important practices. The eight practices developed in this book are not meant to be comprehensive or all encompassing. They are simply the practices emanating from the scriptural book of James, although each resonates deeply with the totality of the biblical narrative. In understanding the purpose of James, however, these eight serve as a solid foundation for a renewed understanding of what it means to discover our identity as disciples of Christ.

Chapter 1

1. Based on J. R. R. Tolkien's book, directed by Peter Jackson, New Line Cinema, 2001. The film portrays this scene with much more poignancy than any similar scene in the novel.

2. Victor Turner and Edith Turner, *Image and Pilgrimage in Christian Culture* (New York: Columbia University Press, 1995) 2.

3. Ibid., 6.

4. Derived from the Greek work *eschaton*, meaning "last," this term refers generally to the study or understanding of the last things. Stanly Grenz helpfully explains eschatology as the conception that "History is directed toward a goal—the Kingdom of God or the presence of the will of God throughout the earth" (*Theology for the Community of God* [Grand Rapids: Eerdmans, 1994] 24).

5. John Bunyan, *The Pilgrim's Progress*, Norton Critical Edition ed. Cynthia Wall (New York: Norton, 2010) 120.

6. Barry Harvey, *Another City* (Harrisburg, PA: Trinity Press, 1999) 26. Regarding his book title, Harvey notes, "The first Christians consistently described themselves as citizen of an *altera civitas*, another city, with a population garnered from every tribe and language, people, and nation" (23).

7. Diana Butler Bass, *Christianity for the Rest of Us* (New York: HarperCollins, 2006) 216.

8. Miroslav Volf and Dorothy Bass, *Practicing Theology* (Grand Rapids: Eerdmans, 2001) 3.

9. The last segment regarding the communal nature of practices comes from Alasdair MacIntyre's definition of a practice. Arguably the preeminent scholar in the philosophy of practice, MacIntyre defined practice this way in *After Virtue*: "By practice I . . . mean any coherent and complex form of socially established cooperative human activity through which goods internal to that form of activity are realised in the course of trying to achieve those standards of excellence which are appropriate to, and partially definitive of, that form of activity, with the results that human powers to achieve excellence, and human conceptions of the ends and goods involved, are systematically extended" (MacIntyre, *After Virtue*, 1st ed. [Notre Dame: University of Notre Dame Press, 1981] 175).

10. Mary McClintock Fulkerson, *Places of Redemption: Theology for a Worldly Church* (New York: Oxford University Press, 2007) 35. In her ethnographic congregational study, Fulkerson notes the way certain practices produce "place." By place, Fulkerson means a good deal more than the generic implication I intend here, incorporating postmodern place theory that suggests place as a gathering of meanings that endures through practices (36), overlapping emergent realities containing residuals of previous times and places (34), and structures of lived, corporate, and bodied experience (25). She suggests such practices are best understood as encompassing Pierre Bourdieu's analysis of *habitus* (*Outline of a Theory of Practice*), meaning that "practices . . . are a social enculturation," or "a bodily knowledge, not caused by principles but done in a way that responds appropriately to a situation; it draws from the past but in an improvisational way" (151).

11. While not printed in time for inclusion in this project, a rich theological account of Christian practices and ecclesiology is offered in L. Roger Owens, *The Shape of Participation: A Theology of Church Practices* (Eugene, OR: Cascade Books, 2010).

12. Samuel Wells, *Improvisation: The Drama of Christian Ethics* (Grand Rapids: Brazos, 2004) 24.

13. I suggest in this book that Christianity offers an ethic distinctive from other systematic attempts to achieve a form of universal morality. Such attempts like utilitarianism, Kant's categorical imperative, religious pragmatism, or some traditional version of natural law tend to result in individualized notions of morality.

Rendering the moral apparatus compatible for everyone places the center of moral development within each person. The individual's rational mind becomes the center of ethical discernment. Therefore, moral judgment and development are taken out of the community and its practices along with the history, context, and narratives that formed that community. Moral deliberation becomes disconnected from other people or history or the stories that form a people.

14. Sam Wells, *Improvisation: The Drama of Christian Ethics* (Grand Rapids: Brazos, 2004) 12, 214. Wells views discipleship, or Christian ethics as he frames it, as an improvisation on the drama told in Scripture. The church performs through practices like those examined in this book as an extension of the story of the Bible, "trusting itself to embody that tradition in new and often challenging circumstances."

15. Stanley Hauerwas and Sam Wells, "How Christian Ethics Was Invented," *The Blackwell Companion to Christian Ethics* (Oxford: Blackwell, 2004) 37. They add, "The narrative is the story of what Christ did and what God did in Christ, and the scriptural narrative shapes and inspires disciples to go and do likewise."

16. Michel de Certeau, *The Practice of Everyday Life*, trans. Steven Randall (Berkeley: University of California Press, 1984) xiii.

17. John Howard Yoder, *Body Politics* (Scottsdale, PA: Herald, 2001) 75. I explore the idea further in chapter 6 of this book.

18. James William McClendon, Jr., *Doctrine* (Nashville: Abingdon, 1994) 367, 334.

19. Diana Butler Bass, *The Practicing Congregation* (Herndon, VA: The Alban Institute, 2004) 66.

20. Bass, *Christianity for the Rest of Us*, 74.

21. Jim Fodor, "Reading the Scriptures: Rehearsing Identity, Practicing Character," *The Blackwell Companion to Christian Ethics* (Oxford: Blackwell, 2004) 150.

22. Tim Conder and Daniel Rhodes, *Free For All: Rediscovering the Bible in Community* (Grand Rapids: Intervarsity, 2009) 187. Conder and Rhodes present a unique and important perspective on reading and interpreting Scripture in the context of the church community rather than with the personal and interpretive techniques often practiced in American churches.

23. Barry Harvey, *Can These Bones Live?: A Catholic Baptist Engagement with Ecclesiology, Hermeneutics, and Social Theory* (Grand Rapids: Brazos, 2008) 161.

24. Harvey suggested that this is the way "scripture (the New Testament) reads scripture (the Old Testament)," *Can These Bones Live?*, 162.

25. Harvey, *Can These Bones Live?*, 163.

26. Bunyan, *Pilgrim's Progress*, 18.

Chapter 2

1. Miroslav Volf, *After Our Likeness: The Church as the Image of the Trinity* (Grand Rapids: Eerdmans, 1988) 129.

2. Paul Minear, *Images of the Church in the New Testament* (Philadelphia: Westminster, 1960). As I have alluded to already, recent scholarship has focused on relating the church to the image of the Trinity (Volf, *After Our Likeness*). Though less biblically explicit than the other images mentioned here, this new Trinitarian ecclesiological conception holds much promise for understandings of the church, local and universal, and therefore for understandings of Christian identity and discipleship. Volf's work holds much influence over the pages of this book.

3. Paul Fiddes, *Tracks and Traces: Baptist Identity in Church and Theology* (Carlisle, UK: Paternoster, 2003) 69.

4. Karl Barth, *Church Dogmatics* 2/2, trans. G. W. Bromiley et.al. (Peabody, MA: Hendrickson, 2010) 666, cf. 661. This christo-ecclesiological perspective is consonant with Barth's christological anthropology and understanding of humanity's covenant-partnership with Christ (see chapter 3, "Participation with God, or The Original (Missional) Church"). Barth claims that the ontological determination of humanity is grounded in Christ's incarnation, that is, Christ's particularity as the one man, Jesus. In simpler terms, Barth understands the essence of human beings to be pre-determined by God taking on human flesh in the form of Jesus. Humanity, from its creation to its redemption, cannot be properly understood apart from its relationship with and in Christ—God who became human. Jesus is present among human beings as the divine other, neighbor, companion, and brother (3/2, 136). Therefore, the essence of humanity is that we are already with God through Christ in our very being. Further, God created human beings to participate in history in which God is at work with humanity and humanity with God, that is, to be God's partner in this common history of the covenant (3/2, 204). The fact of humanity's essence being tied so tightly to the person of Christ from creation makes for an easy transition and understanding of the church community as the historical-earthly form of Christ's existence.

5. Dietrich Bonhoeffer, *Sanctorum Communio: Dietrich Bonhoeffer Works*, vol. 1 (Minneapolis: Fortress, 1998) 138.

6. Dietrich Bonhoeffer, *Christ the Center* (San Francisco: HarperSanFrancisco, 1978) 59. Echoing the famous Reformation debate between Luther and Zwingli, Bonhoeffer argued that in claiming that the church is the Body of Christ, he did not intimate that it merely *signifies* Christ, but actually *is* Christ. Some scholars contend that Bonhoeffer shifted from this strong, literalist ecclesiology later in life as he grew disillusioned with the German Church's complicity with the Nazi regime and the collapse of the Confessing Church originally founded to be an alternative to the Nazified state church. While the reader can certainly see disappointment in

Bonhoeffer's later works, especially his *Letter & Papers from Prison*, there are still glimpses of the strong christo-ecclesiology prominent in his earlier works. One can find such explicit moments in *Ethics* explaining that Christ takes form in the world as the church (New York: Simon & Schuster, 1995, 84). This theme is suggested in various sections of *Letters & Papers from Prison*.

7. Acts 9:2; 19:9; 19:23; 22:4; 24:14; 24:22.

8. While I focus primarily on the images of the church as the Way and as the Body of Christ in this book, I would argue that we need multiple images and conceptual metaphors to attain a full vision of the church—to the extend that we can even do so. While attentive to the multiple images, I focus on the Pauline image of Body of Christ and Lukan image of the Way as the most biblically explicit ecclesiological conceptions. I will keep these two in dialogical tension throughout the book.

9. Stanley Hauerwas and William Willimon, *Resident Aliens: Life in the Christian Colony* (Nashville: Abingdon, 1989) 86.

10. Nigel Wright, *New Baptists, New Agenda* (Carlisle, UK: Paternoster, 2002) 4. In this way the church exists both in space as a Body and in time as an "event." The church "happens whenever the faithful gather, as an apex of the past, present and future" (65).

11. I do not intend for this ecclesiological portrayal to disavow the human dimension of the church, subject to human failings, or lose sight of the complexities of the church's pilgrim existence on earth. In making the theological claim that the church is a set-apart and holy community, I want to acknowledge the tension that exists between the essence of the church as the Body of Christ and the concrete sinfulness of both its members and its corporate action. One only has to look at the Crusades, U.S. congregational segregation, ecclesial Apartheid in South Africa, and the complicity of the German Christian church in the Nazi program, to name just a few of these corporate, ecclesial sins. I hope the ecclesial vision I cast in this book falls not into the traps of ecclesial pride or worse, ecclesial idolatry, but points to the one to whom the church witnesses. That is, it is imperative to remember that the church witnesses to Christ and not to itself. I do not offer a triumphalist account of the church, but a vision of what the church is fully capable of becoming as the Body of Christ, enabled by the Holy Spirit as it develops these crucial pilgrim practices.

12. Paul Fiddes, *Tracks and Traces*, 21. William Bradford recalls the covenanting institution of a local congregation of English separatists in 1607 that would lead to the founding of the first Baptist church under John Smyth.

13. Volf, *After Our Likeness*, 162–63.

14. Discourse on the topic of identity has somewhat fallen out of fashion in academic circles due to escalation in the contentious battles of "identity politics" and fears of accusations of contributing to these battles. Acknowledging that all identities are interlocked and overlapping, I do not wish to deny that what we understand

as orthodox Christian identity is mediated in complicated ways by other cultural, national, and racial contingencies. In calling discipleship foremost an issue of identity, however, I appeal from a christocentric perspective that does not understand discipleship as one ideological identity in political competition with others, but as the foundation of all forms of self—and communal—understanding for those that proclaim Christ as Lord. I seek to avoid reduction into identity politics by claiming that discipleship is not one identity group among others. Instead it permeates all other self-understandings, re-orienting and transforming them toward the pilgrim path of Christ.

15. Emmanuel Katongole, *Mirror to the Church: Resurrecting Faith after Genocide in Rwanda* (Grand Rapids: Zondervan, 2009) 65.

16. Stanley Hauerwas and Samuel Wells, "How Christian Ethics Was Invented," *The Blackwell Companion to Christian Ethics* (Oxford: Blackwell, 2004) 37. Hauerwas and Wells locate Christian ethics—discipleship—within the specific worship practices of the church, from the gathering to the benediction.

Chapter 3

1. The resources written about missional church and missional living are almost countless. Here are a few that offer an overview: David Bosch, *Witness to the World: The Christian Mission in Theological Perspective*; Tim Conder, *The Church in Transition*; Darrel Guder, *The Continuing Conversion of the Church* and *Missional Church: A Vision for the Sending of the Church in North America*; Alan Roxburgh and Scott Boren, *Introducing the Missional Church*; Alan Hirsch, *Forgotten Ways: Reactivating the Missional Church*; Stanley Hauerwas and William Willimon, *Resident Aliens*; Tony Jones, *The New Christians*; most books by Brian McLaren, most books by Leslie Newbigin, and many of the books cited in this project.

2. Karl Barth, *Church Dogmatics* 3/2, 160.

3. Ibid., 204.

4. Recent scholarship in the historical-critical model has shifted to doubt this assertion, crediting the letter to pseudonymic authorship from a follower of James or perhaps another early church leader named James (a popular name during this time). Many believe the writer in James 2 to be responding to Paul's teaching on faith and works, which would place the writing of the letter later than the time of Jesus' brother James, who was executed by the Romans. Also contributing to these doubts is the polished Greek in the letter, considered doubtful coming from a Palestinian Jew of that time. However, one of the more prolific and respected scholars and commentators on the book, and one I reference frequently in this book, Luke Timothy Johnson, advocates for authorship from James the brother of Jesus. Johnson points to the use of early dated Jesus material in the book—considered to pre-date the material used in the Gospels—the lack of title and position embel-

lishment in the letter's introduction, and the use of language and context fitting to a first-generation Christian writer as evidence that the writer is likely, in fact, James the brother of Jesus and leader of the first Jerusalem church (Luke Timothy Johnson, "James," *New Interpreter's Bible* [Nashville: Abingdon, 1998] 183).

5. Robert W. Wall, "Acts," *New Interpreter's Bible* (Nashville: Abingdon, 1998) 222.

6. Alan Roxburgh and Scott Boren, *Introducing the Missional Church* (Grand Rapids: Baker, 2009) 44.

7. Ibid., 103.

8. "The Tutu Connection," *Vanity Fair*, Africa ed., July 2007.

9. Not all contemporary missional descriptions frame the church's mission in terms of participating in the life of God as I have done repeatedly here. In doing this, I follow the work of Paul Fiddes, who works to complement scriptural injunctions to "imitate" God with the pastoral language of participating in God. He suggests in his book, *Participating in God* (Lousiville: Westminster John Knox, 2000) 28, 48–50, that exhortations to imitate God are not adequate. True conceptions of God as Triune must advocate conceiving of God in terms of relationship, correlating to human indwelling in God's "relational spaces." God calls humans to do more than imitate; God calls us to participate with God in the creative and redemptive work of God in the world.

10. Roxburgh and Boren, *Introducing the Missional Church*, 44.

11. John Howard Yoder, *Body Politics* (Scottsdale, PA: Herald, 2001) 21.

12. Dietrich Bonhoffer, *Life Together* (London: SCM, 1949) 58. In this short text, Bonhoeffer posits a daily order that crafts the life of the Christian community into a certain type of political community that understands and offers their life together to Christ as one that is not their own; "to Him [Christ] alone the day belongs" (62).

13. Barna Group, "New Study Shows Trends in Tithing and Donating," 14 April 2008, http://www.barna.org/barna-update/article/18-congregations/41-new -study-shows-trends-in-tithing-and-donating?q=study+shows+trends+tithing +donating.

14. Emmanuel Katongole, *Mirror to the Church: Resurrecting Faith after Genocide in Rwanda* (Grand Rapids: Zondervan, 2009) 52.

15. Molly Marshall translated *koinonia* not as fellowship or communion, but as "participation," reflecting the missional posture of the church community and the pneumatological (i.e., regarding the Holy Spirit) dimension of the community's life together. "We indwell and are indwelt by the lives of others," she asserted. "This is true of our relation to God and to one another," as the Holy Spirit allows us to participate in the life of God and God participates in our communal life (*Joining the Dance: A Theology of the Spirit* [Valley Forge, PA: Judson, 2003] 159).

Chapter 4

1. The Greek verb James uses, translated in the NRSV as "doubt," refers in most Hellenistic usages to making a judgment or conclusion about something (*BibleWorks 7.0: Software for Biblical Exegesis and Research*, BibleWorks LLC, Norfolk VA, 2006). The word connotes a more drastic state than what we often intimate by our expressions of doubts. It seems that James is foreshadowing his discussion of those who are "double-minded" (those with mixed loyalties) in James 4.

2. Christopher Church, "Hebrews-James" *Smyth & Helwys Bible Commentary* (Macon, GA: Smyth & Helwys, 2004) 336.

3. Frederick Buechner, *The Return of Ansel Gibbs* (New York: Knopf, 1958) 303–304.

4. Frederick Danker, ed., *A Greek-English Lexicon of the New Testament* (Chicago: University of Chicago Press, 2000) 817.

5. Karl Barth, *Evangelical Theology* (Grand Rapids: Eerdmans, 1992) 129.

6. See Dietrich Bonhoeffer, *Discipleship: Dietrich Bonhoeffer Works,* vol. 4 (Minneapolis: Fortress, 2001). The book is titled *The Cost of Discipleship* in previous editions. For Bonhoeffer, the disciple's first step—simultaneously the receipt of and response to Christ's call—separates followers from their previous existence and, he added, "immediately creates a new situation." That is, it "creates existence anew" (62). This is not only an epistemological change, but an ontological one as well, meaning not only a change in the way we perceive our situation, but an actual, essential change in our condition as people; the disciple's existence on earth is indelibly altered, converted into a new situation of being that is "separate from the world" (113). The spatial "immediacy with the world" is broken by the temporal immediacy of the call to follow Christ (94), as Christ steps in between the community and the world (95), and a "new state of existence [is] created by obedience" (64). As you can see, Bonhoeffer's work has been instrumental in crafting the thoughts in this project. If you have never read his seminal work on discipleship, put down this book immediately and go read that one!

7. Henri Nouwen, *Wounded Healer* (New York: Random House, 1979) 94.

8. 2 Corinthians 5:17. The NIV translates this verse individually—"If anyone is in Christ, he is a new creation"—while the Greek text references the newness of all creation—the entire world. I have used the translation of John Howard Yoder in *For the Nations: Essays Evangelical and Public* (Eugene, OR: Wipf and Stock: 1997) 39.

Endnotes

Chapter 5

1. Bo Reicke, *The Anchor Bible: The Epistles of James, Peter, and Jude* (Garden City, NY: Doubleday, 1964) 18.

2. Dietrich Bonhoeffer, *Life Together* (London: SCM, 1949) 87.

3. Frederick Danker, ed., *A Greek-English Lexicon of the New Testament* (Chicago: University of Chicago Press, 2000) 326.

4. In describing the "implanted word" in this way, I do not intend to posit a natural law conception of morality. It does not seem this is what James has in mind. It seems that in granting this word salvific power and using such terminology as "truth," "first fruits," and especially "word" (*logos*), James situates the term more christologically or even pneumatologically (i.e, of the Holy Spirit). That is, more than mere conscience, it is the guiding presence of Christ, or Christ through the Holy Spirit, that grants us this divine Word.

5. John Howard Yoder's *Body Politics* contains a chapter on the Holy Spirit working through the congregational meeting to reach consensus among members rather than democratic vote whereby some win and some lose. He points to the unique example of the Quaker meeting (Scottsdale, PA: Herald, 2001, 61–70).

Chapter 6

1. Carol Bailey Stoneking, "Receiving Communion: Euthanasia, Suicide, and Letting Die," *The Blackwell Companion to Christian Ethics* (Oxford: Blackwell Publishing, 2004) 383–84.

2. Howard Thurman, *Jesus and the Disinherited* (Boston: Beacon, 1976) 23.

3. Bo Reicke, *The Anchor Bible: The Epistles of James, Peter, and Jude* (Garden City NY: Doubleday, 1964) 27.

4. Gen 18; Luke 19:1–10; Ruth 1.

5. James bases his injunctions in this passage, especially 2:4, on an Old Testament commandment. In Lev 19:15, the Lord orders the Israelite judges not to show partiality based on economics. They are forbidden from showing favoritism based on whether someone is rich or poor. James utilizes Leviticus 19 several times throughout his short letter, using it as a base on which to build his ethical paradigm.

6. Luke Timothy Johnson, *The New Interpreter's Bible: James* (Nashville: Abingdon, 1998) 192.

7. Richard Hays offers the definitive study on this issue, arguing persuasively for the translation "faith of Jesus Christ," in *The Faith of Jesus Christ: An Investigation of the Narrative Substructure of Galatians 3:1–4:11* (Chico, CA: Scholars, 1983). He contends for a grammatical reading that understands the phrase as a subjec-

tive genitive—faith of Christ—rather than an objective genitive—faith in Christ, noting among other points, that in 23 of 24 other instances of *pistis* followed by a proper noun or pronoun in the genitive case, the genitive is unambiguously subjective (163), and nowhere in the Pauline letters does it constitute an objective genitive (164). The several instances of this construction in Galatians and Romans, he suggests, do not explicitly point to Christ as the object of faith, but place the primary emphasis upon Christ's faith rather than that of the individual believers. Theologically, this representative-christology suggests that Christ's faithful obedience to God is the soteriologically significant event (i.e., what matters for our salvation), vicariously effective on behalf of humankind (167). He is clear to suggest this does not occlude the importance of the individual's belief in in Jesus Christ, but shifts the theological emphasis onto divine faithfulness.

8. Peter Davids, *Commentary on James: New International Greek Testament Commentary* (Grand Rapids: Eerdmans, 1982) 113.

9. Tim Conder and Daniel Rhodes, *Free For All: Rediscovering the Bible in Community* (Grand Rapids: Baker, 2009) 190–93.

10. Dietrich Bonhoeffer, *Discipleship: Dietrich Bonhoeffer Works,* vol. 4 (Minneapolis: Fortress, 2001) 207–8.

11. John Howard Yoder, *Body Politics* (Scottsdale PA: Herald Press, 2001) 28. Yoder explained why ecclesial practices such as baptism, breaking bread, and binding and loosing are ethically formative for Christians. The practice of baptism, for example, breaks down the social, economic, and ethnic barriers that divide people. Just as baptism united Jew and Gentile in a "new humanity," so today it reaches across national and racial boundaries, eliminating social distinctions. To me, this is one of the most important books ever written on congregational practices. (Again, if you have the choice to continue reading my book or to read Yoder's, pick his!)

12. Many scholars believe James had access to material from Jesus' Sermon on the Mount.

13. Donald Kraybill, *The Upside Down Kingdom* (Scottsdale, PA: Herald, 2003).

14. This is both a quotation from Lev 19:18 and from Jesus' direct words in Matt 22:39.

15. James McClendon, *Ethics* (Nashville: Abingdon, 2002) 218.

16. Sara Miles, *Take this Bread* (New York: Ballantine, 2007) 236.

17. Mary McClintock Fulkerson, *Places of Redemption: Theology for a Worldly Church* (New York: Oxford University Press, 2007) 157. In her ethnographic work at Good Samaritan United Methodist, Fulkerson notes how social change requires newly developed habituations; that is, true and lasting change necessitates more than shifting attitudes or dispositions toward those we see as "other" within our midst (i.e., those we see as different from ourselves). It requires intentional (and

perhaps awkward) communal practices of face-to-face relations.This need for face-to-face activities of care and support in congregations contributes to altering social forms of "Othering," whether this othering is based on socioeconomic factors, race, or disability. Her studies portrayed how lasting, redemptive change within that particular congregation required developing "sometimes uncomfortable new habits of being with the other" (157, 248).

18. Yoder, *Body Politics* (Scottsdale, PA: Herald, 2001) 31.

19. Stanley Hauerwas and William Willimon, *Resident Aliens: Life in the Christian Colony* (Nashville: Abingdon, 1989) 17–18.

20. Ibid., 46.

21. William Cavanaugh articulated this distinction well in his work, *Theopolitical Imagination*. He stated, "A public Christian presence cannot be the pursuit of influence over the powers, but rather a question of what kind of community disciples we need to produce people of peace capable of speaking the truth to power" (New York: T&T Clark, 2002, 88). Here I contend with "Niebuhrian" realist notions that seek to exert pragmatic Christian influence and control over the social and moral orders of the state. This seems in some ways a symptom of the epidemic of achievement and urge for efficiency that dominates western society and permeates to theology. This pericope of James, along with other scriptural witnesses, suggests that it is not the task of the church to control the proper political ordering of the world or nation. Rather the church is to proclaim and witness to the inclusive, welcoming gospel of Christ in ways that seek indelibly to alter the world through this communal witness.

22. Miles, *Take this Bread*, 170.

Chapter 7

1. See Dietrich Bonhoeffer, *Discipleship: Dietrich Bonhoeffer Works*, vol. 4 (Minneapolis: Fortress, 2001), which was previously titled *The Cost of Discipleship*. Especially see chapter 1.

2. Brian McLaren, *A Generous Orthodoxy* (Grand Rapids: Zondervan, 2004) 31.

3. Karl Barth, *Church Dogmatics* 4/1, 620.

4. Ibid., 614. Maintaining his christocentric perspective, Barth equates faith with *imitatio Christi*, the imitation of God in the attitude and action of Jesus Christ. It is a correspondence to the faithfulness of God and an imitation of Christ in his humility of obedience to God the Father (634).

5. In verse 14, James asks rhetorically, "Is the faith able to save him?" implying a negative answer. His use of the direct article in Greek, however, indicates he is speaking specifically about the "faith" of the man who *says* he has faith but no

works. That faith, *his* self-proclaimed faith, is not able to save him because it is not true faith. True faith is demonstrated by works. Verse 18 engenders much confusion for scholars, who wonder how many speakers James is employing in this dialogue and what side of the argument he is taking. Regardless of interpretation, James, if nothing else, is certainly reiterating the fact that faith and works are inseparable.

6. Luke Timothy Johnson, *The Letter of James: The Anchor Bible* (Garden City, NY: Doubleday, 1995) 242.

7. Luke Timothy Johnson, *The New Interpreter's Bible: James* (Nashville: Abingdon, 1998) 196.

8. C. S. Lewis, *The Silver Chair, The Chronicles of Narnia* (New York: Harper Collins, 1956) 633.

9. Johnson, *Anchor Bible*, 238.

10. Bo Reicke, *The Anchor Bible: The Epistles of James, Peter, and Jude* (Garden City NY: Doubleday, 1964) 32.

11. Donald Miller, *Blue Like Jazz* (Nashville: Thomas Nelson, 2003) 110.

Chapter 8

1. Bo Reicke, *The Anchor Bible: The Epistles of James, Peter, and Jude* (Garden City, NY: Doubleday, 1964) 39.

2. This story can also be found in Tony Campolo, *Let Me Tell You a Story* (Nashville: W Publishing Group, 2000) 111–12.

Chapter 9

1. Luke Timothy Johnson, *The Letter of James: The Anchor Bible* (Garden City NY: Doubleday, 1995) 243–44 and Christopher Church, "Hebrews-James," *Smyth & Helwys Bible Commentary* (Macon, GA: Smyth & Helwys, 2004) 364.

2. Frederick Danker, ed., *A Greek-English Lexicon of the New Testament* (Chicago: University of Chicago Press, 2000) 562; Francis Taylor Gench, *Hebrews and James* (Louisville: Westminster John Knox, 1996) 115.

3. Donald Miller, *Searching for God Knows What* (Nashville: Thomas Nelson, 2004) 92.

4. Dietrich Bonhoeffer, *Discipleship: Dietrich Bonhoeffer Works*, vol. 4 (Minneapolis: Fortress, 2001) 85.

5. Brian Walsh and Sylvia Keesmaat, *Colossians Remixed: Subverting the Empire* (Downers Grove, IL: Intervarsity, 2004) 177.

Endnotes

6. Walter F. Adeney, *The Greek and Eastern Churches* (Edinburgh: T & T Clark, 1908) 400–401.

7. Gregory A. Boyd, *The Myth of a Christian Nation* (Grand Rapids: Zondervan, 2005) 144–45.

8. John Howard Yoder, *The Politics of Jesus* (Grand Rapids: Eerdmans, 1972) 38.

9. Gench, *Hebrews and James*, 116.

10. The story comes from Timothy Tyson's autobiographical book on the challenges of growing up as the son of a white minister in the prejudiced South, *Blood Done Sign My Name* (New York: Three Rivers, 2004) 73–81. The direct quote is from page 81.

Chapter 10

1. Margaret R. Miles, "Image," *Critical Terms for Religious Studies*, ed. Mark C. Taylor (Chicago: University of Chicago Press 1998) 160.

2. Sondra Ely Wheeler, *Wealth as Peril and Obligation: The New Testament on Possessions* (Grand Rapids: Eerdmans, 1995) 101.

3. Ralph Martin, "James," *Word Commentary* (Waco TX: Word Books, 1988) 174.

4. Christopher Church, "Hebrews-James," *Smyth & Helwys Commentary* (Macon GA: Smyth & Helwys, 2004) 415. Statistics are from the National Priorities Project, http://www.bread.org/hunger/us/facts.html; http://www. bread.org/hunger/global/facts.html.

5. An important Latin American advocate for this "preferential option" from a position of Scripture is Gustavo Gutierrez.

6. Wheeler, *Wealth as Peril and Obligation*, 98.

7. Quoted in Church, "Hebrews-James," 390.

8. Shane Claiborne and Jonathan Wilson-Hartgrove, *Becoming the Answer to Our Prayers* (Downers Grove, IL: Intervarsity, 2008) 34–36. For a fuller telling of the story with biblical antecedents, see Claiborne and Chris Haw, *Jesus for President: Politics for Ordinary Radicals* (Grand Rapids: Zondervan, 2008). While you're at it, check out Claiborne's first book as well, *The Irresistible Revolution*.

9. Leviticus 25 declares that every fifty years, at the sound of a ram's horn, the Israelites were to celebrate Jubilee. After seven Sabbath-years—when the land was left fallow for the entire year—on the fiftieth year God proclaimed liberty to everyone throughout the land as all economic and social disparities from the past fifty years are undone and society is restored to an egalitarian state. Israel is called to "proclaim liberty to all inhabitants"—that is, emancipate all Hebrew slaves, in-

cluding those who sold themselves into slavery to pay off an economic debt. God enjoined every Hebrew to return to his and her homeland as all land is returned to its original owner. Those who lost land due to debt or exploitation gain assurance of the return of that land in the Jubilee. They are also to return to their families, implying that those sold into slavery were to be released to begin anew in Hebrew society. In addition, all debts are canceled. God calls each Israelite to pardon the debts owed them as they let the debtor-slaves go free, a practice made more explicit in Deut 15:1–18. Finally, God commands all sowing, harvesting, and reaping of the fields prohibited. Israel will eat off of what the land has previously produced.

The people of God are called to a radical structuring of society through the Jubilee. It is a time for new beginnings as slaves and poor return to their original God-given land. The oppression of debt is lifted and the danger of social hierarchy subsides as the people celebrate together the God of freedom. God desires Israel to embody an alternative community, to live according to a different ethic from the rest of the world in all of its social and economic interactions. This radical command becomes a major theme in the message and life of Jesus. Theologian John Howard Yoder, among others, points out how this practice shapes the message of Jesus. The "acceptable year of the Lord" proclaimed by Jesus, as he read from the scroll of Isaiah in the Nazareth synagogue, is a reference to the Year of Jubilee (Luke 4:16–21). In this passage, as Jesus stated his mission and pronounced it fulfilled, he called his followers to Jubilee by saying the good news of God is the liberation offered in the Jubilee (John Howard Yoder, *The Politics of Jesus* [Grand Rapids: Eerdmans, 1972]). Yoder argues that the Jubilee ought to be a guide for the normal, everyday practices of Christians.

10. Ralph Martin, "James," *Word Commentary* (Waco, TX: Word, 1988) 184.

11. *BibleWorks 7.0: Software for Biblical Exegesis and Research*, BibleWorks LLC, Norfolk, VA, 2006.

12. Richard Hays, *The Moral Vision of the New Testament* (New York: Harper Collins, 1996) 343.

13. Church, "Hebrews-James," 404.

14. Martin Luther King Jr., "A Time to Break Silence" [among others], *A Testament of Hope: The Essential Writings and Speeches of Martin Luther King Jr.*, ed. James M. Washington (New York: HarperOne, 1986). This sermon, delivered at Riverside Church in New York City in 1967 during the middle of the Vietnam War, was one of the first occasions on which King linked the war to the civil rights movement and the movement for economic equality. While "defense" spending has decreased proportionally since the mid-1980s, some groups contend that nearly 50 percent of federal revenue spending (excluding designated taxes like social security and Medicare, etc.) is spent on the military. Other groups place the number at one-quarter of federal expenditures, depending on whom you ask (i.e., which party or lobbyist group, and how they calculate it). See the 2009 federal budget breakdown

from the National Priorities Project, showing that military expenditures (military, military interest on debt, and veterans benefits) constitute 35.4 percent of federal spending (http://nationalpriorities.org/en/ publications/pdf-viewer/taxday-2010/). Some reports suggest the federal defense budget nearly equals the entire military spending of the rest of the world.

15. From Father George Zablka's speech, "Blessing the Bombs," given at the *Pax Christi* Conference, August 1985, quoted in Claiborne and Haw, *Jesus for President*, 222–23.

16. See http://www.usatoday.com/news/washington/2006-02-02-bono-transcript_x.htm.

Chapter 11

1. Universal Pictures & Dreamworks, 2001.

2. Stanley Hauerwas, "Memory, Community, and the Reasons for Living: Reflections on Suicide and Euthanasia," *The Hauerwas Reader* (Durham, NC: Duke University Press, 2001) 583.

3. These churches carry on an ancient tradition dating from church origins. Early church history contains many recordings of miraculous healings where anointing and healing rituals were regular ecclesial practices.

4. Christopher Church, "Hebrews-James," *Smyth & Helwys Commentary* (Macon, GA: Smyth & Helwys, 2004) 411.

5. This body/soul dualism in many ways predates Enlightenment thought, originating in the Platonic philosophy of Hellenistic Judaism. The Enlightenment brought about a resurgence in this pattern of thinking from the "less sophisticated" beliefs of the Middle Ages.

6. Frederick Danker, ed., *A Greek-English Lexicon of the New Testament* (Chicago: University of Chicago Press, 2000) 982.

7. Dietrich Bonhoffer, *Life Together* (London: SCM, 1949) 106.

8. Miroslav Volf, *After Our Likeness: The Church as the Image of the Trinity* (Grand Rapids: Eerdmans, 1988) 148.

9. Karl Barth, *Church Dogmatics* 4/1, 460.

10. Ibid., 449.

11. Barth, *Church Dogmatics* 3/2, 197.

12. These points regarding "freedom" are ones that liberation theologians know well and ones that I, a white American theologian and minister, would do well to heed.

13.Evelyn Brooks Higginbotham describes this phenomenon within many black churches as "the black church as a public sphere." Since African-Americans were denied access to public space following a mass removal of blacks from American public life during Reconstruction, "the black church—open to both secular and religious groups in the community—came to signify a public space, the one true accessible space for the black community." The black church serves as the public space where a people caught in the story of oppression and injustice "regrouped and rallied against emotional and physical defeat." Higginbotham proposes that the black church historically constitutes a "multiple site," an institution embodying all the needs of and caring for a community under oppression. "The Black Church: A Gender Perspective," *Righteous Discontent* (Cambridge: Harvard University Press, 1993) 3, 7. Mary Patillo-McCoy calls the black church an "encompassing institution," noting its historical role of encompassing all the needs and public expressions of the community. "Church Culture as Strategy of Social Action in the Black Community," *American Sociological Review* 63 (1998).

14. John Koenig articulates these points much better than I do in his chapter on "Healing" in *Practicing Our Faith*, edited by Dorothy C. Bass. The incarnation of God becoming human and the Christian doctrine of bodily resurrection break down the Enlightenment walls dividing the ethereal from the tangible. Because the concept of "embodiment" is so central to the Christian faith—God taking on human form, the church community making up the Body of Christ, bodily resurrection in the *eschaton*—it is impossible to understand healing and redemption in any way other than as a physical and spiritual event. God's mission to redeem and make new all of creation renders any dichotomy between physical and spiritual false.

Afterword

1. Emmanuel Katongole, *Mirror to the Church: Resurrecting Faith after Genocide in Rwanda* (Grand Rapids: Zondervan, 2009) 69.

2. T. S. Eliot, "Little Gidding," from *Four Quartets* (New York: Mariner, 1968).

3. Dietrich Bonhoeffer, *Discipleship: Dietrich Bonhoeffer Works*, vol. 4 (Minneapolis: Fortress, 2001) 251.

Index of Names and Subjects

Index of Names and Subjects

Index of Scripture References

Index of Scripture References